Boasting a long history and rich cultural content, traditional Chinese opera, or *xiqu*, is one of the world's three major ancient theatrical cultures, with the other two being ancient Greek drama and Indian Sanskrit drama.

Appreciating

Traditional

Chinese

Compiled by: Mei Weidong ,Mei Wei

Photo Assistant: Wang Zijian

Translated by: Ma Rui

Polished by: Dorian Cave

新 星 出 版 社　NEW STAR PRESS

Opera

Contents

PRELUDE
A Splendid Legacy of *Xiqu*, or Traditional Chinese Opera[①]

Boasting a long history and rich cultural content, traditional Chinese opera, or *xiqu*, is one of the world's three major ancient theatrical cultures, with the other two being ancient Greek drama and Indian Sanskrit drama.

Chinese opera originated from primitive songs and dances and evolved by combining a mixture of folk songs and dances, ballad singing and burlesque. The rather developed operatic art we see today, which consists of over 360 different styles, took shape during the Song and Jin dynasties around a thousand years ago, assimilating the essence of various art forms, including literature, music, dancing, fine arts, martial arts, acrobatics and performing arts. Therefore, a major characteristic of traditional Chinese opera is their integration of a number of different

---

① One difficulty that arises when discussing traditional Chinese opera in English is the difficulty in choosing an adequate translation for the Chinese word *xiqu* (戏 曲). Various translations include "theatre of song", "music drama" and "opera", but none of these really conveys the correct meaning, and most attempts will confuse an English-speaker who is already familiar with Western meanings associated with the words *theatre, music, opera, drama* and *play*. Most Westerners, though, have some concept of "Chinese opera" (most commonly defined historically by "Peking Opera") as being quite different from any of these. For this reason, the term "traditional Chinese opera" is a good start for a translation of *xiqu*.

Xiqu, or traditional Chinese opera

art forms with a shared criterion, so that the operatic art, as a unique art form, actually reflects the influence of all the above art forms.

The earliest mention of the term *xiqu* is in a book entitled *Biography of the Poet Wu Yongzhang*, by Liu Yun (刘埙, 1240-1319) of the Song Dynasty. The so-called "Yongjia *xiqu*" he mentioned in the book actually referred to the "southern opera" or *nanxi*, *xiwen* (literally "skit") and "Yongjia *zaju*" (literally "variety show") also mentioned by people of later ages, with Yongjia being a county in the southeast of Zhejiang Province, roughly today's Wenzhou. It was only during the Republic of

An old-style operatic stage

China era that Wang Guowei (1877-1927) began to use *xiqu* as the generic term for traditional Chinese opera.

Generally speaking, for all ancient civilizations around the world, the rudiments of artistic elements were integrated during the "pre-artistic period" (or the period of primitive religion). In the European continent, various artistic forms gradually took shape in the next stage of development. Consider the Greek drama, for example. In ancient times, songs and dances had their place in the drama, while after the theatrical reforms advocated by Sophocles, Euripides and other dramatists, songs and dances gradually lost their importance, and dialogues and body movements predominated. Later on, the poetic dialogues were gradually replaced by dialogues in vernacular language; consequently, the verse drama declined, and modern drama took form. On the other hand, songs and dances followed their own paths of development and won a place

Wrestling dance

Canjun xi (adjutant play) of the Tang Dynasty

Paiyou, literally "comedians"

in the field of theatrical arts in the forms of opera and dance drama, respectively.

The case is totally different for the traditional Chinese opera, which is always an art form integrating songs, dances and acting. From the performances of *paiyou* (俳优), literally "comedians," of the Qin and earlier Han dynasties, considered by some as the rudiment of Chinese *xiqu*, the traditional Chinese opera experienced a development of over a

Operatic stage performance

Traditional Chinese opera

thousand years through *baixi* (百戏, literally "hundred shows," including acrobatics, sword swallowing and other circus performances) in the Han Dynasty and *canjun xi* (参军戏, or "adjutant play") in the Tang Dynasty, to *nanxi*, or "southern drama," in the late Song dynasty and *yuan zaju*, "miscellaneous drama," in the Yuan Dynasty. In order to lay out the rich and colorful social life of the time within the confined space of the stage, and in order that ordinary people, who lived quite a monotonous everyday life, experience excitement and stimulation of the senses when watching the plays, Chinese *xiqu* artists of successive generations assimilated the essence of many other art forms, including poetry, music, dancing, painting, ballad singing, acrobatics and martial arts, and made it a strikingly inclusive form of art with a great many splendid varieties to catch the eyes and imagination of the audience. In other words, the traditional Chinese opera developed into an art form characterized by dialogues, singing and body movements, by giving full play to various artistic elements including literature (folk ballad singing), music and dancing and allowing a seamless integration of all those elements.

All dialogues rhyme in Chinese opera, and the body movements of actors and actresses follow a dancing rhythm. We all know that singing and dancing come from life and extend beyond life; that is to say, the reality rendered in these performances is exacerbated and enhanced. This is even more in the case of Chinese theatrical art. In order to emphasize

Prop weapons of traditional Chinese opera

and dramatize everyday language, movements and emotions, the facial make-up, costumes and body movements of actors and actresses all have a texture of pretension and affectation. To this end, generations of Chinese thespians have made painstaking efforts to polish the performing techniques of singing, speaking, acting and acrobatic fighting in Chinese opera, and have finally created and developed a series of extremely stylized and formalized compositional and choreographic rules. In the traditional Chinese opera, all actors and actresses are bound by prescribed methods for every single kind of physical action pertaining to human behavior. When performing the action of "laughing," for example,

Traditional Chinese opera roles

The facial make-up (*lianpu*)

he or she must make a series of exaggerated, expressive and stylized moves, which remains true even today. Exaggerated and exacerbated as they are, all conventionalized stage techniques in the traditional Chinese opera find their source in everyday life. It is through their astute observation and comprehension of people's subtlest movements in their everyday life that Chinese theatrical artists developed those rules to express the physical and personal charm of dramatic characters, so as to achieve perfection in both form and soul.

Beyond performing techniques, the facial make-up (*lianpu*) and costumes, including embroidered robes, hairdressing, pheasant plumes, "water sleeves," beards and thick-soled boots, as well as a wide variety of grotesque stage props are also enlarged and exaggerated, and one must follow strict conventions in using each of them. These props effectively enhance the aesthetic appeal of theatrical performances thanks to their striking beauty in shape and colors, and have been widely accepted and popular among the Chinese audience.

Why, then, does the traditional Chinese opera seek this exacerbation of reality even in the minutest expression of actors and actresses? There might be many ways to explain this, but obviously, among the most important factors is the fact that Chinese operatic troupes sought to entertain the majority of people from all walks of life in the society through commercial performances, and that their social status was relatively low, so that they had to cope with poor financial standing in carrying out their performances. In ancient China, the venues of operatic performances were usually barnyards, temples or any open area, and in the countryside, theatrical troupes often set up a stage in the busy and noisy marketplace. In order that their performances would not be overwhelmed by the hurly-burly of the crowded mass, performers had no choice but to seek effective methods to build and strengthen their own presence among the audience. It is for this purpose that they eventually established the artistic rule of rendering reality in an extremely exaggerated manner: loud singing to the powerful sound of gongs and drums, picturesquely embroidered costumes, rich and colorful facial make-up, long beards swinging gracefully in the vehement acrobatic fighting scenes. This technique proved effective in creating great aesthetic appeal and attracting the interest of the audience; more importantly, by making use of all these formalized and conventionalized stage techniques

A traditional pose

Traditional Chinese opera performers

in an expressionistic and abstract style, traditional Chinese operas achieve a perfect balance between the real and the fantastic, the lively acting and the dramatic structure, the rigorous routines and the freedom of expression.

Thus we see that traditional Chinese operas fully acknowledge theatrical virtuality and never pretend to realness; on stage, the artists constantly shift between the real and the imagined, the physical and the virtual. This is totally different from — and even contrary to — the artistic principle of theatrical illusion, as practiced by Western theatrical artists.

In Western theatre, from the moment the curtain is drawn, the dramatists make use of every possible stage technique to create an illusion of reality, so that the audience can gradually forget that they are watching a play, and become engrossed in the atmosphere and ambience created on the stage as if they were personally experiencing everything that is happening. To this end, Western dramatists make the stage a geographically bounded and relatively fixed space, and with such stage settings as paintings and stage props, they try to create inviting scenes within which characters develop and dramatic conflicts are resolved. In each scene, the passage of time in the dramatic plot approximates the actual performance time as perceived by the audience. Such is the spatiotemporal concept characteristic of Western theatre, which is based on Aristotle's theory of art as imitation; indeed, he attributed the origin of art to the human affinity for imitation, and in this view, the criterion to evaluate art is whether it reflects human life in an accurate manner.

Traditional Chinese theatrical artists do not regard imitation of reality as their purpose; they create no illusion of reality through stage techniques, nor do they seek the agreement of space and time on the stage through any actual spatiotemporal distribution in reality. In traditional Chinese theatre, there is almost no setting on the stage. The stage setting is actually established through the characters' activities; in other words, the stage in itself is nothing but an abstract space without these activities. The temporal pattern of traditional Chinese theatre is not relatively fixed, either, but extremely abstract and flowing, or rather extremely "flexible," for the temporal length is established at the absolute discretion of dramatists, and is entirely determined by plot development.

Why has traditional Chinese theatre survived and flourished, despite such an abstract and flowing spatiotemporal pattern? For a simple reason: everything on the Chinese stage is created by the stylized and precise performance of the actors. The distribution of space and time as prescribed in the play script is actually achieved by the actors' performance, which is tacitly understood and acknowledged by the audience.

Besides the virtuality of theatrical rendition, this specific

Different masks of traditional Chinese opera

spatiotemporal pattern of traditional Chinese operas also has something to do with the stage mechanism featuring the continuous entrance and exit of characters. Actors come onto the stage from the entrance door and go off through the exit door, but these seemingly simple movements are quite significant in the Chinese theatre, for they represent a stage mechanism totally different from the Western one, in which separate

Performance of *Female Generals of the Yang Family* (*yang men nü jiang*)

acts are structured with different settings. It is through the entrance and exiting of characters that the transformation of dramatic scenes is achieved, and that plot development is driven. Consider the Peking Opera play *Female Generals of the Yang Family* (*yang men nü jiang*,《杨门女将》) for instance. In the midst of resounding gongs and drums, Mu Guiying, fully armored and armed, comes onto the stage from the entrance door, bold and brave, and it is tacitly understood by the audience that the character is now in the drill ground and training her soldiers. Then the actor goes through the exit door to the barracks. This mechanism featuring the characters' moving onto and off the stage, together with the basic skills of performers — including singing, recitation, acting and acrobatic fighting — as well as the musical accompaniment by the band, effectively present the spatiotemporal and atmospheric changes of the plot, so that the stage appears as an unfolding painting scroll. Within a single scene of a play, the environment may easily change along with the characters' activities. When the character waves his whip and speaks: "I have traveled a distance of a thousand *li* and my horse has passed so many mountains," the audience immediately understands that he has traveled a long distance and that his geographical location has already changed.

Now that we know it is the performers' artistic creation that constructs the free-flowing spatiotemporal pattern in traditional Chinese theatre, how can we explain this? I believe the core reason lies in the fact that the traditional Chinese stage is endowed with a whole set of techniques of expression featuring virtuality.

Without any stage setting or prop, a performer can make known to the audience the immediate surroundings of the character s/he impersonates, using nothing but her/his meticulous gestures and body movements depicting the events and atmosphere around. For example, in the Huai opera play *Love in the Wardrobe* (*gui zhong yuan*, 《柜中缘》), the performer makes it immediately obvious to the audience what the character is doing by her/his conventional but delicate hand movements of threading, knitting, stitching and embroidering, even though s/he is not actually holding anything in her/his hands. Besides impersonating physical scenes and objects through her/his body movements, the performer also aims to convey the character's psychological and emotional state through this method of depiction. In this sense, the theatrical art of expression featuring virtuality perfectly blends physical, psychological and emotional aspects of dramatic characterization.

The virtuality feature of traditional Chinese theatre gives playwrights and performers considerable artistic freedom, and greatly enhances performance expressivity within the confined physical space of the stage. Thanks to their outstanding performing techniques, performers manage to take the audience on a journey into their shared imagination of a

whole range of situations and scenes, whether it is an odyssey through mountains and rivers or a fierce and deadly battle scene; as a result, the artistic creation actually reaches its complete form in the imagination of the audience. This is the way in which traditional Chinese theatre can recreate real-world conditions and the various aspects of human life.

Nevertheless, one should keep in mind that although this is an effective strategy to expand the imaginary space of the stage, the performance is not free from restrictions; instead, it is bound by the basic rule of any artistic endeavor, namely, that art should be a reasonable rendition of reality. Therefore, virtuality on the traditional Chinese stage is integrated with the sense of reality conveyed by the performance. In traditional Chinese opera there is a whole set of stylized movements imitating the act of riding a horse, called *tang ma* (趟马), in which there is no horse on the stage; but the performer wields a real horsewhip; her/his movements of flipping the whip and spurring the horse are accurate and rigorously conform to the well-established theatrical routines, and these moves are in accordance with the logics that govern everyday life. For example, in the Peking opera play *Stealing the Imperial Horse* (*dao yu ma*,《盗御马》), the character Dou Erdun glories in his successful revenge after having stolen the horse, and this state of mind is reflected in the performer's *tang ma* movements; in *The Sister-in-Law Heroines* (*gu sao ying xiong*,《姑嫂英雄》), the character Xue Jinlian, as a young

tang ma movements

girl, is very intent on saving the lives of the emperor and her father, and the character's eagerness and conceitedness also appear in the performer's *tang ma* movements. As mentioned above, traditional Chinese theatrical art does not pretend to accuracy by imitating physical, temporal and geographic reality, but focuses on mimicking the movements made by people in their everyday life, and the finest actors can blend the real and the false in a seamless and beautiful way through their excellent performance, so that the movements and states of mind of the characters on the stage are immediately understood by experienced Chinese theatre-goers.

CHAPTER I
Delicate and Elegant Kunqu Opera:
Ancestor of Chinese Opera

Kunqu opera, originally known as "Kunshan tunes" or "Kun tunes", is the oldest extant form of Chinese opera. It has been called *"Kunqu"* (literally "Kun melodies") since the Qing Dynasty, and nowadays it is also called *Kunju* ("Kun opera"). As one of the oldest surviving musical and theatrical traditions of the Han people in China, Kunqu opera is considered the finest of Chinese cultural traditions, especially in the realm of traditional Chinese opera. It is thus called "the orchid in the garden of Chinese opera," for the Chinese see this flower as the embodiment of pure and delicate beauty.

The History of Kunqu Opera

Kunqu opera enjoys a centuries-long history. As early as the late Yuan and early Ming dynasties (the mid-14th century), more than 600 years ago, Kunqu emerged in the Kunshan area (then under the jurisdiction of Taicang Prefecture) of today's Jiangsu Province. Ever since the Song and Yuan dynasties (10th-14th centuries), there has been a divide between southern and northern traditions of Chinese theatre, and even within the southern tradition, there is a great diversity of tunes and singing styles according to different geographic areas. At the time, the most well-known operatic tunes in the southern tradition were the Kun tunes, Haiyan tunes and Yuyao tunes originating in the Zhejiang area, as well as Yiyang tunes originating in the Jiangxi area — collectively called the Four Major Kinds of Operatic Tunes of the Ming Dynasty. In the late Yuan Dynasty, Gu Jian and a few others began to collect and improve the southern tunes that were popular in the Kunshan area, and his improved tunes were originally called "Kunshan tunes", the rudiment of today's Kunqu opera. At first, the Kunshan tunes were no more than small musical pieces and songs, sung by people in Suzhou and the surrounding area. It was in the Ming Dynasty, under the reign of Emperor Wanli (1573-1620), that Kunshan tunes began to spread from Suzhou to the areas south of the Yangtze River and north of the Qiantang River; gradually they were

A painting of an ancient stage of Kunqu opera

disseminated to the Fujian, Jiangxi, Guangdong, Hubei, Hunan, Sichuan, Henan and Hebei areas, and began to be sung in Beijing near the end of the Wanli era. In this way, the Kunshan tunes became China's most influential set of operatic tunes and form of opera during the period from the mid-Ming Dynasty to the mid-Qing Dynasty.

During the reign of Emperor Jiajing (1522-1566), Wei Liangfu, an outstanding operatic musician, made some important innovations to the tones and singing style of Kunshan tunes. He brought the gentle and flowing beauty of the Kunshan tunes into full play, while at the same

Kunqu opera characters

time integrating the best features
of other southern tunes as well
as the rigorous structure of
northern operatic traditions into
Kunshan tunes. He adopted the
singing techniques of northern
tunes and chose the *di* (Chinese
flute), the *xiao* (vertical bamboo
flute), the *sheng* (a reed pipe
wind instrument) and the
pipa (four-string pear-shaped
Chinese lute) as accompanying
instruments, thus creating a new
operatic genre called *shui mo
diao* (floating water mill tunes,
水磨调), which became generally

A Kunqu opera show

known as "Kunqu."Liang Chenyu, a native of Kunshan, carried forward
the achievements of Wei Liangfu, by studying and further improving the
Kun tunes. Thanks to Liang's innovative efforts, the Kun tunes began
to be sung with a simple instrumental accompaniment, which helped
their clear and beautiful melodies to stand out much more than when
accompanied by loud percussion instruments. In order to give more

strength to the Kun tunes, Liang worked on traditional southern tunes, in which the main musical instruments were the *xiao* and the *guan* (a pipe wind instrument), and adopted the *di*, the *guan*, the *sheng*, the *qin* (a seven-string plucked string instrument), the *pipa* and the *xianzi* (another plucked string instrument) to form a band accompanying the tunes, which proved to be a great success. During the last year of Emperor Longqing's reign (1572), Liang Chenyu composed the first "romance play" of Kunqu opera, entitled *Washing the Silken Gauze* (*huan sha ji*, 《浣纱记》). The play was such a triumph that Kunqu opera became widely popular, especially among the literati, for whom composing Kunqu opera "romance plays" became a fashion. An increasing number of people learned to sing Kunqu opera, especially female singing entertainers or singing courtesans (*geji*). An example of this is Chen Yuanyuan, a notorious courtesan in Chinese history, famed for her skill at singing Kunqu opera.

As mentioned above, Kunshan tunes were originally sung by people in Suzhou and the surrounding area, spread south of the Yangtze River and north of the Qiantang River during the reign of Emperor Wanli, then gradually spread to the Fujian, Jiangxi, Guangdong, Hubei, Hunan, Sichuan, Henan and Hebei areas. Near the end of the Wanli era, it had arrived in Beijing via Yangzhou, surpassing all other operatic tunes and becoming the standard operatic tunes for romance plays. "All songs sung nationwide find their origin in the Wu area," to quote a popular saying

Kunqu opera

of the time. Then at the end of the Ming Dynasty and the beginning of the Qing Dynasty, Kunqu opera further spread to the Sichuan, Guizhou and Guangdong areas, and became a national form of opera. At first, the Kun tunes were sung in the Wu dialect of Suzhou, but after this art form was disseminated nationwide, people from various geographic areas began to sing the Kun tunes in their own dialects, to the sound of their own folk music; as a result, many new schools of Kun tunes emerged, collectively forming a rich and colorful system, and making Kunqu a form of opera representative of the Chinese nation as a whole. During the Qing Dynasty, Kunqu opera further developed and became even more widespread thanks to Emperor Kangxi's great interest in it, and the opera witnessed its most glorious days during Emperor Qianlong's reign (1736-1795). To conclude, Kunshan tunes became the most influential set of operatic tunes, and remained the dominant form of Chinese opera from the mid-Ming Dynasty to the mid-Qing Dynasty. 600 years later, Kunqu opera is not only the oldest extant form of opera in China, but also that with the longest history in the world.

According to scholarly studies, although the aesthetic principles of Kunqu opera obviously originated in the southern area of China, especially south of the Yangtze River, technically it does not stand for the local culture of any specific area; it is rather an embodiment of the aesthetic pursuits and artistic creativity of literati from all over China.

It was only because it represented the refined taste of the literary class that Kunqu opera was able to spread beyond the boundaries of the southern regions, and maintain a consistent style in the process of its dissemination.

As the most influential set of operatic tunes and form of opera from the mid-Ming to mid-Qing dynasties, Kunqu indeed had a great influence on many traditional Chinese operas, to such an extent that it is regarded as the "ancestor" of all Chinese operas. Throughout the history of traditional Chinese theatre, Kunqu opera is the one with the longest history, the richest legacy of plays and the most complete system of performances. It is a brilliant cultural heritage of the Han people of China, and thus holds an important position in the history of Chinese literature, theatre, music and choreography.

Artistic Characteristics of Kunqu Opera

Characters and Role Categories in Kunqu Opera

At its earlier stage of development, Kunju belonged to the system of southern opera, and thus it inherited the role categorization of the southern operatic system, but it also assimilated the fine traditions of *zaju* (variety show) of North China, from which it inherited seven basic

Different Kunqu opera roles

1	**2**	**3**
4	**5**	

1. *Wu dan* (the fifth-rank *dan* role, also called *gui men dan*) character
2. *Tie dan* character
3. *Si dan* (the fourth-rank *dan* role, also called *ci sha dan*) character
4. *Chou* character
5. *Lao dan* character (left-hand side)

role categories, namely those of *sheng* (male roles), *dan* (female roles), *jing* (roles with a painted face), *mo* (middle-aged male roles), *chou* (clowns), *wai* (seniors with white beards) and *tie* (female supporting roles). The Kunqu play *Huan Sha Ji* mentioned above represented the role categorization of the earlier stage of Kunqu; that is, besides the above seven basic roles, there were also *xiao mo* and *xiao dan* roles borrowed from *zaju* of the Yuan Dynasty, and three additional roles, *xiao sheng, xiao wai* and *xiao jing* (in all these five roles, *xiao* means "young"), so there were altogether twelve role categories in the play.

At the height of the popularity of Kunqu, at the end of the Ming Dynasty, in *Mohan Zhai Adapted Version of Romances* (《墨憨斋定本传奇》), the Ming edition of a collection of romances compiled by Feng Menglong (1574-1646), we can see that the "old woman" impersonation role of *tie* had changed into the role of *lao dan,* which shows the influence of the Yuan Dynasty *zaju,* while other role categories remained the same as that of the earlier stage. It is well-known that until the reign of Emperor Kangxi, Kunqu opera still comprised twelve role categories.

During Emperor Qianlong's reign, one-act plays (*zhezi xi*) of Kunqu opera were extremely popular, and performing techniques were further enhanced. To facilitate better characterization, some new breakthroughs were enacted as regards role categorization for this form of opera. In the 1795 book *Profile of Yangzhou Life* (*yang zhou hua fang lu,* 1795, 《扬

州画舫录》) there was a mention of "twelve lines of business", including seven male role categories: *fu mo, lao sheng, zheng sheng, lao wai, da mian, er mian* and *san mian;* four female role categories: *lao dan, zheng dan, xiao dan, tie dan;* and one comic role category known as *"za."* Later, following the evolution of Kunqu opera in south China, *xiao sheng* and *dan* gradually became two major categories, and even more detailed subdivisions sprung up under these two categories. Specifically, under the category of *xiao sheng* the roles were subdivided into *da guan sheng, xiao guan sheng, jin sheng, xie pi sheng* (also called *qiong sheng*) and *zhi wei sheng*, and under the category of *dan* the roles were subdivided into *lao dan, zheng dan, zuo dan* (occasionally young boy roles), *si dan* (the fourth-rank *dan* role, also called *ci sha dan*), *wu dan* (the fifth-rank *dan* role, also called *gui men dan*) and *liu dan* (the sixth-rank *dan* role, also called *tie dan*). But different schools of Kunqu opera included different role categories and subdivisions.

With the development of Kunqu opera, this role categorization became increasingly more complex. In the Qing Dynasty, under emperors Jiajing and Daoguang, the "twelve lines of business" in Kunqu opera integrated even more specific subdivisions, so that a total of twenty subdivisions were established under the five major role categories, namely *sheng, dan, jing, mo* and *chou;* there were twenty role subdivisions in Kunqu at this stage.

Photos of Kunqu opera

A *zhi wei sheng* (pheasant tail male role) character of Kunqu opera

The category of *sheng* was further subdivided into *guan sheng, jin sheng, xie pi sheng* and *zhi wei sheng*, representing different types of character roles. Performers in the line of *guan sheng* (官生, literally "official male roles") impersonate male adults who have become officials, and the role can be further divided into *da guan sheng* (senior official male roles, 大官生) and *xiao guan sheng* (junior official male roles, 小官生) according to the age and official ranks of characters. For example, the character of Emperor Ming of the Tang Dynasty (唐明皇) in the play *The Palace of Eternal Youth* (*chang sheng dian,*《长生殿》) and that of Li Bai in the play *Drunken Li Bai Writing a Poem* (*tai bai zui xie,*《太白醉写》) are both performed by actors in the line of senior official male roles, while Wang Shipeng in *A Tale of the Wooden Hairpin* (*jing chai ji,*《荆钗记》) and Pan Yue in *A Tale of the Golden Sparrow* (*jin que ji,*《金雀记》) are played by performers in the line of junior official male roles. The parts of *guan sheng* and *jinsheng* (kerchief male roles, 巾生) are different. *Jin sheng* is the male role of cultured and genteel young scholars, and therefore the singing style swings back and forth between chest voice and falsetto, with more use of the latter, making the tunes more clear and melodious to the audience. *Guan sheng* is the male role that is more free and easy in singing and performing style; to play the role of *da guan sheng,* the performer must have an imposing manner, and chest voice and falsetto are also used alternatively in the singing, but when singing in chest voice, the pitch is higher than that of *jin sheng* roles, thus making the sound loud and sonorous. *Xie pi sheng* (鞋皮生, shoe leather male role) is a category for poor and unconventional young male roles, and they are so called because being poor and having no official rank, these young males usually wear dirty and tattered shoes; to the south of the Yangtze River, they are known as *"tuo xie pi."* The *zhi wei sheng* (pheasant tail male roles, 雉尾生) is a warrior whose helmet is decorated with the feather from a pheasant's tail, and it is also called *ji mao sheng* (鸡毛生, chicken feather male roles) or *ling zi sheng* (翎子生, pheasant plume male roles). Performers in this line of business have a loud and powerful voice, master the skills of acrobatic fighting, and are skillful in playing with pheasant plumes.

As far as vocabulary is concerned, there are six subdivisions under the *dan* role category, namely *lao dan, zheng dan, zuo dan, si dan,*

Zheng dan character

Liu dan (the sixth-rank *dan* role, also called tie *dan*) character

wu dan and *liu dan*, but in practice there is another subdivision, *tie dan*. The *lao dan* (老旦, senior female roles), also called *lao tie dan* (老贴旦, senior female supporting roles), is a senior female role originally performed by a female actress at the time when Kunqu first appeared, but since women were forbidden to perform on stage under the Qing Dynasty, this role was generally performed by male actors thereafter. *Lao dan* roles usually wear simple make-up without any thick paints, and male performers playing this role wear headdresses. *Zheng dan* (正旦, starring female roles) are usually married women from relatively lower social class, whose performance displays such qualities as honesty, naturalness and

Guan sheng (male official) character

Lao sheng character

poise. The singing style of *zheng dan* performers shows more vigor and strength, with loud and sonorous sound. There is a rich legacy of plays starring this role category, in which a large variety of characters with distinct characteristics provide large room for performers to give full play to their performing techniques. *Zuo dan* (作旦) is also called *hua sheng* (花生, boy *sheng* roles), *wawa sheng* (娃娃生, little boy *sheng* roles) or *wawa dan* (娃娃旦, little boy *dan* roles). Roles in this line are mainly young boys under the age of 15. These roles were originally placed under the category of *tie dan* (贴旦, supporting female roles). The *si dan* (四旦, fourth-rank female role) is also called *ci sha dan* (刺杀旦),

Xie pi sheng (鞋皮生) character. Poor and lacking any official rank, this kind of young males usually wear dirty and tattered shoes

Zuo dan character. This subdivision under the category of *dan* is also called *hua* sheng (boy *sheng* roles)

and can be further subdivided into the *ci dan* (刺旦, assassinating female roles) and the *sha dan* (杀旦, killed female roles), from whose names we can see that performers in this line of business should be skilled in body movements and acrobatic fighting. *Ci dan* roles correspond to female assassinators seeking revenge, and are often played by *zheng dan* performers; as for *sha dan* roles, they correspond to female characters who are killed for their mercilessness and immorality, and they are often acted by *zuo dan* or *tie dan* performers. The *wu dan* (五旦, fifth-rank female role) is also called *gui men dan* (闺门旦, young unmarried female role), and performers in this line of business often impersonate unmarried young girls, whose performance emphasizes singing and body movements, as they showcase the reserved, graceful and charming aspect of young ladies; this role subdivision is a common feature of romantic plays. The *liu dan* (六旦, sixth-rank female role) has several alternative names, including the *tie dan*, the *xiao dan* (小旦, younger *dan* role), the *feng yue dan* (风月旦, petty *dan* role), the *kuai le dan* (快乐旦, happy *dan* role) and the *huo po dan* (活泼旦, lively *dan* role), etc. Performers in this line of business often impersonate smart, witty and resourceful young girls from the lower class, such as maids, little girls, young ladies, and country women.

There are two divisions in the role category of *jing*, or "painted face": *da mian* (大面, literally "big face") and *bai mian* (白面, literally "white face"). The facial make-up for *da mian* is relatively simple, mainly featuring red and black colors, as is told in an old Kunqu opera proverb: "[There are] seven red faces, eight black faces and three monk faces" (*qi hong ba hei san he shang*, 七红八黑三和尚). The "seven red faces" and "eight black faces" refer to two Kunqu plays, *A Tale of Seven Red Faces* (*qi hong ji*, 《七红记》), in which the faces of seven godly characters are painted red, and *A Tale of Eight Black Faces* (*ba hei ji*, 《八黑记》), in which the faces of eight godly characters are painted black.

As for the "three monks," they stand for three monk characters [Lu Zhishen in *Monastery Main Gate* (*shan men*,《山门》), Yang Wulang in *Wutai Mountain* (*wu tai shan*,《五台山》) and Monk Huiming in *Delivering a Letter* (*xia shu*,《下书》)]. Performers in the line of *bai mian* usually impersonate villains, whose faces are painted white except for eye sockets, and this role is further subdivided into *xiang diao bai mian* (相貂白面, fur hat white face), *zhe zi bai mian* (褶子白面, robe white face) and *duan shan bai mian* (短衫白面, short dress white face), among others. Sometimes, "white face" performers impersonate heroes or neutral characters, and sometimes they also impersonate female characters. In the *la ta bai mian* (邋遢白面, untidy white face) subdivision, the performer's face is painted white, but also has black lines painted around the eyes and nose. These are usually lower-class characters or comic characters.

In the role category of *mo* (末, middle-aged male role), the subdivisions are those of *lao sheng* (aged male role), *mo* and *lao wai*. In Kunqu opera, there is no division between civil and military roles in the line of *lao sheng*, examples of which include Lin Chong in *A Tale of the Double-edged Sword* (*bao jian ji*,《宝剑记》) and Qin Qiong in *The Qilin Pavilion* (*qi lin ge*,《麒麟阁》).

In the role category of *chou* (clowns) there are two subdivisions, *fu* (also called *er mian*, literally "second-rank patched face") and *chou*. In

Kunqu opera

the case of performers of *fu* roles, the white patch painted on their face covers the corners of their eyes near the temple, while for those of *chou* roles, the white patch only covers the face under the middle of their eyes; another difference is that *fu* characters wear robes and official garments, while *chou* characters wear short garments. The subdivision of *fu* did not exist in the southern opera or *zaju* of the Yuan Dynasty; by introducing this new role subdivision under the category of *chou*, in Kunqu opera plays, characters under this line of business began to include those from upper-class society, since *fu* performers often impersonate dishonest scholars, treacherous court officials, wicked lower-class officers, evil law practitioners and hangers-on of the ruling class. The characteristics shared by all these characters are their treachery and deceitfulness, and the performers must show the coldness of these characters, which is why this role subdivision is also called "cold-water *er mian*" (*leng shui er mian*, 冷水二面). Due to the fact that the white patch on the face of *chou* characters is smaller than that on the face of *fu* characters, the *chou* subdivision is also called "*xiao hua lian*" (小花脸, smaller white patch), and since it is a role subdivision that follows "*er mian*", it is also called "*san hua lian*" (三花脸, third-rank white patch), representing characters from the lower-class society or lovable comic characters, such as the tea master in *A Tale of Searching for the Relatives* (*xun qin ji*, 《寻亲记》), Wan Jiachun in *The Happiness of the Fisherman's Family* (*yu jia le*,

《渔家乐》) and others. There is no division between civil and military roles in the line of *chou*, and some *chou* performers may have to perform a fair amount of acrobatic fighting.

Eighteen performers are generally enough to form a traditional professional troupe of Kunqu opera, which gave rise to a popular saying according to which "eighteen headdress sets are enough to perform an opera." Few large-scale troupes have twenty-seven performers to represent all the above lines of business, given the fact that generally speaking, when a troupe has actors representing ten role categories, it can already organize a performance — indeed, the characters from other role categories can be played by performers of similar roles. These ten basic role categories, the so-called "ten pillars of the troupe," are *jing, guan sheng, jin sheng, lao sheng, mo, zheng dan, wu dan, liu dan, fu* and *chou*, among which the preeminent ones are *jing* (painted face), *lao sheng*(aged male roles), *guan sheng* (official male roles) and *zheng dan* (starring female roles).

Music, Recitation, Tunes and Band of Kunqu Opera

Musical structure is the most fundamental aspect of music in traditional Chinese opera. There are two main styles of musical structures: *lian qu ti* (联曲体, "joined song style", also called *qu pai lian tao ti*, 曲牌联套体, literally "joint set of fixed melodies"); and *ban qiang*

Traditional Kunqu moves

Characters of Kunqu opera

ti (板腔体, "beat-and-tune style", also called *ban shi bian hua ti*, 板式变化体, literally "changing metrical-type style").

The *lianquti* structure is employed in the *xiqu* music of playwright-centered musical systems: Kunshan tunes and Yiyang tunes. Following this musical structure, vocal music is derived from a large number of "fixed melodies" (*qupai*, 曲牌), usually arranged in a specific order. Each fixed melody conveys both emotional and structural meaning. In creating new plays, playwrights first select and arrange fixed melodies, then write lyrics to fit them. Operatic forms employing this playwright-centered compositional process tend to be more elitist. Kunqu is the principal extant form of opera in this system, and it is the opera that makes the most rigorous use of this system. According to incomplete statistics, there are over a thousand fixed melodies employed by Kunqu opera. Their origins vary, from ancient melodic singing and dancing music of the Tang and Song dynasties to *chang zhuan* (唱赚) and various types of music that were popular in the Song Dynasty, as well as folk music and songs of ethnic minority groups, etc. Musical composition in Kunqu was based on southern tunes while borrowing the systems of northern tunes, and artists employed various compositional techniques in traditional Chinese music.

Qu pai, or fixed melodies, constitute the most basic unit of musical tunes in Kunqu opera. According to Wu Mei (1884-1939), a musicologist specializing in the theory of traditional Chinese music in the Republic of China period, there were over 4,000 fixed melodies in the southern tunes system and over 1,000 in that of northern tunes, but among these, only 200 were commonly used. Some of the most popular melodies in the southern tunes include *bu bu jiao* (步步娇), *zao luo pao* (皂罗袍) and *hao jiejie* (好姐姐) sung in the play *A Walk in the Garden* (*you yuan*, 《游园》), as well as *lan hua mei* (懒画眉) and *chao yuan ge* (朝元歌) from *Flirting by Zither Playing* (*qin tiao*, 《琴挑》). Both plays are commonly used to train performers to grasp basic performing techniques — in fact, as a rule, female performers of Kunqu opera start learning from *A Walk in the Garden* and male performers start from *Flirting by Zither Playing*.

By employing fixed melodies, composers of Kunqu music joined different melodies and formed a joint set of fixed melodies (also called "song cycle", 套数). The selection of different fixed melodies and the formation of varied sets thus constituted the music and literary structure of the entire play. Generally a play would feature a unique set of fixed melodies.

The musical and lyrical structures of fixed melodies are consistent. The *qu pai* actually originated from the *ci*, a form of classical Chinese poetry featuring lines of uneven length, which explains why the *qu pai* are also called *ci yu* (词余). The lyrics are actually written as *ci*

Kunqu opera band

poems, and for each *qu pai*, there are fixed rules concerning how many characters should there be to each line, how many lines to the entire poem, and which phonetic tones (level or oblique) should be used for each character. Certain melodies make it necessary to follow strict rules regarding the oblique tones (rising or falling-rising tone), to prevent hindering musical composition and the performers' singing. Therefore, it is by no means an easy task to compose and sing Kunqu opera.

As far as the singing style is concerned, in Kunqu opera the emphasis is placed on a clear articulation of the words in the rendition of operatic tunes, and the singers are to follow strict rules in singing

A Kunqu performance: *The Peach Blossom Fan*

these tunes. Contrary to other traditional operas, in which singers may have more freedom based on their own voice, performers of Kunqu opera must follow fixed melodies, fixed tunes, fixed rhythms and fixed music scores. The tunes of Kunqu opera are extremely beautiful and elegant, particularly sweet and lingering to the ear. Performers pay high attention to the control over their voice and tones in singing Kunqu, and the rhythm of music and articulation of lyrics are exquisite, with the accompaniment of a full musical band.

As is mentioned above, *shui mo diao* (floating water mill tunes), a significant singing style of Kunqu opera, was given full expression in the slow tunes ("fine tunes") of the southern tunes system. The rhythm is deliberately slowed down, so that the singer may add more ornamental trills and runs in his or her singing. Besides the commonly-used "one strong beat and three weak beats" (*yi ban san yan,* 一板三眼, which corresponds to the quick and simple 4/4 of Western music) and "one strong beat and one weak beat" (*yi ban yi yan,* 一板一眼, which corresponds to the 2/4 of Western music), there is *zeng ban qu* (赠板曲, tunes with octuplet time), meaning 4/4 melodies being slowed down into an 8/4 beat, which makes the music extremely clear, soft and lingering. Besides, strict rules must be followed in the articulation of each character of the lyrics, and for each character, great attention must be paid to its exact pronunciation and tone during the entire singing process, since the musical nuances can be extremely subtle for each character, and it is in the minute changes of tones and tunes that the sweetness and lingering of the singing style are emphasized.

Comparatively speaking, the northern tunes feature free and easy rhythms, and they employ the seven-note musical scale, which makes it different from southern tunes that employ the five-note musical scale (with no semitones). But throughout their long development, the Kunshan tunes assimilated the style of northern tunes and integrated their style with the latter, so that in the repertoire of Kunqu opera, we can see individual fixed melodies and joint sets of fixed melodies drawn from northern tunes, and occasionally we can even see joint sets of fixed melodies from both southern and northern tunes, hence the so-called "*nan bei cheng tao*" (南北成套, song cycles of melodies from both south and north). In the use of this style, which integrates both southern and northern tunes, there are also rules to be followed. Generally speaking, melodies drawn from northern tunes are sung by one character, and those from southern tunes, by several characters. Naturally, the integrated style is chosen according to the plot of every specific play — which is to say that in the operatic art, music is used to build, promote and enhance the drama of the play.

Concerning singing techniques, performers of Kunqu opera pay attention to the control of their own voice, the rhythm of the music

Characters of Kunqu opera

and the clear and exact articulation of the lyrics, and there are different tuning rules and strict rules for each character type to represent the traits of that type. As for the rhythm of Kunqu music, besides the above-mentioned *zeng ban qu* which slows down 4/4 melodies into an 8/4 beat, for both southern and northern tunes, there are commonly used "one strong beat, three weak beats," "one strong beat, one weak beat," flowing rhythms and free rhythms. There is much diversity in the use of all these rhythms, but generally speaking, all must be used to serve the plot and characterization of the plays.

Within Kunqu opera, recitation also has its special characteristics. Since Kunju originated in the Kunshan area of Wuzhong (today's southern area of Suzhou), the speaking style naturally displays characteristics of the soft dialect of Suzhou. Characters in the *chou* category also

A character of Kunqu opera

use local dialects from the Suzhou area in their recitation, such as *Su bai* (speaking in local Suzhou dialect) and *Yangzhou bai* (speaking in Yangzhou dialect). These dialects are widely used by local people of the lower class; they are full of life, and the recitation also features language which is rhymed to the fast rhythm timed by an instrument resembling a rapid clapper.

The band structure of Kunqu opera is well established, generally comprising three sections: pipe instruments, string instruments and percussion instruments. The major instruments is the *di* (Chinese flute), together with the *sheng* (a reed pipe wind instrument), the *xiao* (a vertical bamboo flute), the *sanxian* (a three-string instrument) and the *pipa* (a four-string pear-shaped Chinese lute). The use of the *di* — which makes a very soft and distant sound — as the major accompanying instrument, together with the *zeng ban qu* rhythm, the clear and slow articulation of lyrics, as well as the gentle and flowing beauty of the Kunshan tunes due to the influence of Wuzhong folk songs, all contribute to making Kunqu music the finest among all traditional Chinese operas for its sweet melodies and soft tonal quality. Many fixed melodies from the musical accompaniment were widely borrowed by other local operas.

Kunqu Opera Performance

A Kunqu opera performance involves a whole set of rigorous routines, which lay special importance on singing and dancing.

Kunqu is best known for its emphasis on lyricism and exquisite postures, as well as on its skillful integration of singing and dancing movements. Indeed, Kunqu opera is an artistic form involving multiple performing skills, such as singing, dancing, body movements and recitation. The integration of singing and dancing is particularly exemplified in the posture routines followed by performers in each "line of business." The body movements in Kunqu opera can be divided into two categories: one is the auxiliary postures of performers as a body language and the dancing moves developed from gestures; the other is the lyrical choreography that accompanies the singing. In a word, the body movements in Kunqu opera are in themselves a beautiful choreography, and they constitute an effective way to represent the state of mind of characters and clarify the meaning of the lyrics sung to the music.

Kunqu opera dancing assimilated and inherited the traditions of ancient folk dances and court dances. Through long-term practice on the stage, Kunqu artists have accumulated a rich experience in integrating songs and recitations with dances, and created many dancing movements with the purpose of depicting the drama and settings, and these movements designed to build and propel the plot thus became an important element of narrative one-act plays. On the other hand, in order to meet the needs of plays emphasizing both lyricism and action, many lyrical dances were also created, which became major performing skills in lyrical one-act plays. Well-known plays in this category include *The Map of the Western Sichuan — The Reed Pond* (*xi chuan tu · lu hua dang*,《西川图·芦花荡》), *A Tale of Loyalty and Patriotism — Sweeping Qin Hui with A Broom* (*jing zhong ji· sao qin*,《精忠记·扫

秦》), *The Moon Worshiping Pavilion — Stepping on the Umbrella* (*bai yue ting· ta san,*《拜月亭·踏伞》), *A Tale of the Double-Edged Sword — Fleeing at Night* (*bao jian ji·ye ben,*《宝剑记·夜奔》), *A Tale of Interlink Stratagem— Questioning the Spy* (*lian huan ji·wen tan,*《连环记·问探》) and *The Ferocious Pellets — The Mountain Kiosk* (*hu nang tan · shan ting,*《虎囊弹·山亭》).

The Kunqu Opera Repertoire

Bringing a Single Broadsword to the Armed Banquet (dan dao hui,《单刀会》)

The plot of *dan dao hui*, a story from the *Romance of the Three Kingdoms*, revolves around Guan Yu's attending the banquet arranged by Lu Su, and coming back safe and sound thanks to his wit and bravery. During the period of the Three Kingdoms, Lu Su invites Guan Yu for a banquet, leading Guan to suspect it is an ambush aiming at coercing him to concede the strategic area of Jingzhou to the State of Wu. Lu even asks Sima Hui, an old friend of Guan Yu's, to attend the banquet and drink with Guan, but Sima Hui refuses and warns Lu Su not to act rashly. Guan Yu, fully aware of Lu's intention, accepts the invitation and goes to the banquet with only one man, Zhou Cang, to accompany him, and

1, 2. A performance of *Bringing a Single Broadsword to the Armed Banquet* (*dan dao hui*)
3, 4, 5. A performance of *The Peony Pavilion* (*mǔ dan ting*)

a single broadsword; as he leaves, he bids Guan Ping and Guan Xing, his fellow generals, to wait for him at the riverside. During the banquet, Lu is defeated in a battle of wits against Guan, and is so impressed by Guan's eloquence and bravery that he dares not carry out his plan of ambushing him. As a result, Guan Yu leaves the banquet safely.

The purpose of this play is not to tell a story, nor is it to portray complex and ever-developing characters. Here the playwright merely aims at expressing his admiration for certain historical heroes, and from a larger perspective, he can also be understood to convey the despondence of a suppressed people at a time of acute conflicts between historical enemies. The arias written for both Guan Yu and Sima Hui express this kind of feeling, and they are similar in both content and tunes. It is noteworthy that there is very little development of dramatic conflicts in this play, and the body movements of performers are rather slight and exquisite. The ending of the play is actually foreshadowed and stated in the first three acts: the first two acts foreshadow the final defeat of Lu Su, and in the third act Guan Yu explains his strategies through his recitation. By ensuring the audience is aware of everything that has happened, is happening and will be happening, this technique encourages all spectators, from the very beginning, to pay less attention to plot development or dramatic tension, and instead engross themselves in the emotional and psychological experience of the characters in the play. The playwright's goal is to encourage empathy, on behalf of the audience, with the feelings of the characters — and in a sense, with his own.

The Peony Pavilion (mu dan ting, 《牡丹亭》)

This is a long play of fifty-five scenes that focuses on the love story of Liu Mengmei, a young student, and Du Liniang, the daughter of a high official in Nan'an, southern Jiangxi. During a visit to the family garden at the back of her father's official residence, Du Liniang falls asleep and is approached in a dream by a young scholar, Liu Mengmei, and has an affair with him in the Peony Pavilion. Awakened from her dream, she becomes lovesick; inconsolable, she pines away and falls ill in the seclusion of her maidenly chamber. Before she dies, she has someone paint a portrait of herself, and buries it under a stone in the garden. Her remains are later placed nearby, beside a plum tree. Shortly afterwards, Governor Du is transferred to a military post in northern Jiangsu. Before the family departure, provision is made for sacrifices to her spirit tablet in a shrine in the garden.

In the meantime, Liu Mengmei, on his way from Guangdong to attend the imperial examination held in Hangzhou, falls ill at Nan'an and is told to rest at the summer house in the Dus family garden. The discovery of the girl's portrait leads him to spend many hours longing for her, and gazing fondly at her lovely face. But eventually his wishes are

A performance of *The Peony Pavilion* (*mu dan ting*)

granted: one night, she appears to him, and they renew their relationship born in the dream. At her bidding, the coffin is opened, and she is found there alive, as fresh and beautiful as ever. The couple then leaves for Hangzhou, where Liu Mengmei takes the imperial examination, but there is a delay in the proclamation of the examination results due to a national crisis caused by the invasion of northern Jiangsu by a rebel leader allied with the Jurchen Tartars. Worried by the news of the war that has spread to her father's district, Du Liniang sends her husband to look for the latter, taking her portrait as identification.

By this time, Governor Du has already cleverly quelled the rebellion.

A performance of *The Peony Pavilion* (*mu dan ting*).

In celebration of the victory, his subordinates offer him a feast. The happy event, however, is disturbed by the arrival of Liu Mengmei, who claims to be the Governor's son-in-law. Having been told previously of the alleged profanation of his daughter's grave, Governor Du suspects an imposture and foul play. Instead of recognizing Liu as his son-in-law, he has him arrested, and Liu Mengmei is given a sound whipping in the governor's office, before he is rescued by an official in search of the scholar come out first in the imperial examination.

Finally, in an audience before the throne, Liu Mengmei proves his claims with the help of his resurrected wife. The play ends, as usual, with an official promotion, along with family reconciliation and reunion.

A timeless masterpiece written by Tang Xianzu (1550-1616), a great dramatist from the Ming Dynasty, *The Peony Pavilion* is a romance that shares with Shakespeare's *Romeo and Juliet* the intent to celebrate the magic and power of youthful love; both plays also exalt the capacity of love to conquer ossified social conventions. Upon its first production, *The Peony Pavilion* was very controversial because of its views on women, sex, and marriage. While women were supposed to be submissive at the time, the heroine, Du Liniang, is a strong woman who actively pursues the man she loves, which explains why this dramatic character has become the most charming one in classical Chinese literature after Cui Yingying in *The Tale of the West Chamber* (*xi xiang ji*). In a culture given to conservative views about sexual relations, the story is remarkable for its strong and erotic undertones. And in a society where arranged marriages had been the norm for centuries, the story flies in the face of convention by having the young lovers united in a marriage based on love and decided by themselves, without any outside intervention. The play is well-known for its elegant and ornate literary style, its witty and interesting recitation, and its tunes that integrate the bold and vigorous style of the northern tunes and the delicate and lingering style of the southern tunes. Lü Tiancheng (1580-1618), a Ming Dynasty opera critic, regarded *The Peony Pavilion* as "the best of all [operas] in history for its soul-stirring and cleverly developed plot and artistic fineness."

Fifteen Strings of Cash (shi wu guan, 《十五贯》)

The story of *shi wu guan* takes place in the Ming Dynasty. You Hulu, a butcher, borrows fifteen strings of cash from a relative to make a living. Back home, he plays a practical joke on his step-daughter, Su Xujuan, claiming that he got the money by selling her into slavery. Hearing this, Su escapes from home late at night. Later on, Lou Ashu, a gambler, creeps into You's house and steals the fifteen strings; afraid of being caught, he kills You with a butcher's knife. Discovering the murder, You's neighbors report to the official and begin hunting the murderer. As a parallel story line, Xiong Youlan, a shop clerk working for the rich merchant Tao Fuzhu, meets Su Xujuan on his way to Changzhou with fifteen strings of cash to make purchases, and the two of them start to travel together because they are heading for the same destination. When You's neighbors and some official clerks encounter them, in possession of fifteen strings of cash, they take them for You's murderers; hearing this, Lou Ashu seizes the opportunity to plant false evidence against them. Su Xujuan and Xiong Youlan are thus arrested and sentenced to death by the county magistrate of Wuxi. However, the Governor of Suzhou, Kuang Zhong, feels there is something amiss, and orders that the case be reexamined. In the process, Kuang travels personally to the scene of the crime, dressed up as a fortuneteller. He fools Lou Ashu, and thus arrests him as the real murderer.

While the original play was written by Zhu Suchen, a Qing Dynasty playwright, the version performed today is an adaptation by Chen Jing based on Zhu's play and on the story *Fifteen Strings of Cash* from Feng Menglong's *Lasting Stories to Awaken the World* (*xing shi heng yan*, 《醒世恒言》). It was performed for the first time by the Zhejiang Kunqu Opera Troupe in 1956.

In January 1956, the Guofeng Kunqu Opera Troupe made a successful debut in Hangzhou with their performance of *shi wu guan*. This play, also known as *The Tale of the Two Xiong Brothers* (*shuang xiong ji*, 《双熊记》), criticizes the subjective and stiff judgment of bureaucratic officials, and praises the practice of seeking the truth from facts.

In April 1956, *shi wu guan* was put on stage in Beijing. On April 17, Mao Zedong watched this play in the Huairen Hall of Zhongnanhai, and generously praised the themes of the play and the performance itself. On April 19 Zhou Enlai also watched the performance and met all performing crew, whom he praised as having "rescued a form of opera from obscurity. *Shi wu guan* shows great sympathy for working-class people, and it is of fine artistic taste." On May 17 of the same year, over 200 figures from Beijing cultural circles were invited by the Ministry of Culture and the China Dramatists Association to attend a symposium on the Kunqu

A performance of *Fifteen Strings of Cash* (*shi wu guan*)

play *shi wu guan* in Ziguang Hall, Zhongnanhai. Zhou Enlai made an appearance, and gave a one-hour-long speech. He honored Kunqu opera as "an orchid of the south," and praised the newly-adapted play *shi wu guan* as "a successful adaption of a classical play" and a good example illustrating the principle of "giving arts a free expression and producing innovating artistic works to suit the new age." On May 18, a *People's Daily* editorial penned by Tian Han was published, entitled "Talking about 'A Single Play Rescuing a Form of Opera from Obscurity'" — and Kunqu and *shi wu guan* thus became hot topics in the mass media and among the general public.

The Palace of Eternal Youth (*chang sheng dian*, 《长生殿》)

This play was written by Hong Sheng (1645-1704) in the early Qing Dynasty, based on the long Tang Dynasty poem "The Everlasting Regret" (*chang hen ge*, 《长恨歌》) by Bai Juyi (772-846), and on the Yuan Dynasty play *The Rain on the Phoenix Trees* (*wu tong yu*, 《梧桐雨》) written by Bai Pu (1226-1306). It tells the love story which takes place between Li Longji, Emperor Xuanzong of the Tang Dynasty, and his favorite concubine, Yang Yuhuan. In this play, Hong Sheng added extra texture to the original story, in order to make the love story even more enticing, but also to provide a more elaborate overview of this story's social and historical background.

When Yang Yuhuan becomes the Emperor's favorite consort, he gives her two love tokens: a gold hairpin, and a casket adorned with gold-leaf flowers. Her older brother Yang Guozhong becomes Chancellor of the Right. Banished once for a fit of jealousy, she regains favor by sending the Emperor her shorn locks as a token of her love. A frontier general, An Lushan, is sent to the capital to be punished for an offense, but Yang Guozhong obtains a pardon for him, thereby winning a promotion and a princely title for himself. A military man, Guo Ziyi, who has come to the capital to receive an appointment, witnesses from a wine house window the extravagant pomp and splendor enjoyed by the Yang family and An Lushan.

After challenging the power of Yang Guozhong, An Lushan is exiled from the capital by the Emperor. He stirs up a rebellion, and Guo Ziyi trains his troops to counter the imminent rising. Oblivious of this situation, Emperor Xuanzong and Lady Yang bathe together in a hot spring, and on the seventh day of the seventh month, the "lovers' night" in the traditional Chinese culture, they make a sacrifice to the Herd Boy and Spinning Damsel star gods, vowing eternal love for each other. When An's forces menace the capital, Xuanzong departs with his entourage towards the relative safety of Sichuan. On the way, at Maweipo, his mutinous troops, blaming the Yangs for their plight, kill Yang Guozhong and demand Lady Yang's death. Helpless, Xuanzong allows her

A performance of *The Palace of Eternal Youth* (*chang sheng dian*)

to hang herself, and she is provisionally buried there. An Lushan usurps the imperial throne, and takes over the capital. Xuanzong, grieving for Lady Yang, places a portrait of her in a Sichuan temple, and worships and weeps before it. Meanwhile, moved by the plight of Lady Yang's forlorn soul, the Spinning Damsel persuades the Jade Emperor of Heaven to permit Lady Yang to become an immortal in the paradise of Penglai. She also gives Lady Yang liquid jade and liquid gold to pour on her corpse, thereby reuniting body and soul.

A performance of *The Palace of Eternal Youth* (*chang sheng dian*)

Imperial power is transferred to Emperor Suzong, Xuanzong's son, who sends Guo Ziyi to quell the rebellion. Guo succeeds, and the two emperors head back to the capital. When he passes through Maweipo, Xuanzong can find no trace of Lady Yang's body — only her perfume sachet. Back in the capital, he dreams that Lady Yang has sent for him, and thereafter commands the Taoist necromancer You Tong to seek out Lady Yang's soul. Aided by the Spinning Damsel, the Taoist reaches Penglai, where Lady Yang gives him half of the gold hairpin and part of the casket to take to Xuanzong as tokens of renewed love. On the appointed date, You Tong sets up a fairy bridge to the Moon Palace, and sends Xuanzong alone to the moon. There, the two lovers are blissfully reunited, and thanks to the Spinning Damsel's efforts, are commanded by the Jade Emperor to dwell forever as husband and wife in the paradise.[①]

By adding social and political events to the royal life of the major characters, the story gained several twists and turns. Hong Sheng asked his friend Xu Lin, a musician from Suzhou, to compose the music in strict accordance with the fixed melodies, so that the entire opera has quite a well-established musical structure very well suited to the dramatic characters and settings. Being drunk, Yang Yuhuan sings the melodies of *The Candle-Drawn Moth* (*bu deng e*, 《扑灯蛾》) with a distinctive southern style, presenting to the audience the vivid picture of a drunken imperial concubine. Guo Ziyi, on the other hand, expresses his indignation through strong and vigorous northern tunes. It is this seamless integration of northern and southern styles that has made this

① http://en.wikipedia.org/wiki/The_Palace_of_Eternal_Life..

play such a great success ever since its debut; and it is said that when it was performed, people in the capital of Beijing were very enthusiastic about singing the melodies from the play. Some of the passages have been adapted by artists of other local operas, an example of which is the Peking opera play *The Drunken Beauty* (*gui fei zui jiu,*《贵妃醉酒》) performed by Mei Lanfang, a world-famous Peking opera master.

CHAPTER II
**Appealing and Amazing Peking Opera:
the Outstanding Representative of Traditional
Chinese Opera**

The History and Development of Peking Opera

Known as the quintessence of the Chinese operatic art, Peking opera is one of the most delightful artistic traditions of China, and it remains a fascinating window from which foreigners may glimpse the brilliant culture of this great nation. Peking opera has a history of merely 160 years, but this operatic form represents an integration and a refinement of various local operas. Bringing them to a higher level, Peking opera inherits and carries forward the outstanding artistic features of traditional Chinese opera.

The Birth of Peking Opera

People are now used to describing the most prosperous period of the Qing Dynasty as the "Golden Age of Emperors Kangxi, Yongzheng and Qianlong" ("*kang qian sheng shi*"). This was indeed a period of economic prosperity and political stability at the end of China's feudal history, which left ample room for cultural development. It was during this period of time that Peking opera began to take shape, and it remains to this day the most brilliant pearl of traditional Chinese opera.

At the beginning of the Qing Dynasty, the traditional Chinese opera kept on thriving in the same way it had been in the previous dynasty. During the reigns of emperors Kangxi and Qianlong (these two emperors

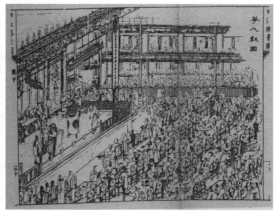

| 1 | 3 |
| 2 | |

1. Emperor Kangxi (1654-1722)
2. Emperor Qianlong (1711-1799)
3. A celebration of the 80th birthday of Emperor Qianlong

are usually mentioned alone to refer to this prosperous period, due to the fact that Emperor Yongzheng's reign in between only lasted for a short 13-year period of time), Chinese society experienced a prolonged period of economic prosperity and social progress. First of all, these are basic social and economic conditions necessary to the development of traditional operas, and secondly, social well-being created higher demand for

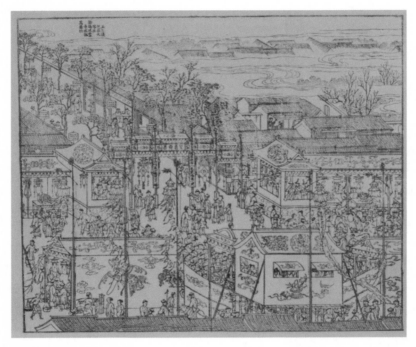

Painting depicting the Anhui operatic troupes coming to Beijing to celebrate Emperor Qianlong's 80th birthday

outstanding plays. At that time, Beijing was China's political, economic and cultural center, so that a huge number of performers specializing in various operatic tunes and local operas came and gathered there, starting in the Qianlong period. Teahouses and theatres were built everywhere in the capital city; high-level officials and wealthy people even built stages within their own houses, and employed operatic troupes to give

Peking opera play *The Drunken Beauty* (*gui fei zui jiu*)

performances for their families during festivals or grand occasions. Since most officials and wealthy families had their houses built within the inner city, theatres where ordinary people could watch operatic shows were located in the outer city, but they were extraordinarily bustling whenever performances took place: the streets were crowded with theatre-goers, and this brought much business to the neighboring restaurants. People would talk about the performers in the restaurants, and they would even sing some lines of the plays for fun. It was the so-called *"luan tan* period" (乱弹期) in the history of traditional Chinese opera, during which two new systems of operatic tunes started to rise — namely the *bangzi* and the *pihuang*, which competed with the former two major systems, the Kun tunes and the Yiyang tunes.

Yiyang tunes were also known as "capital tunes" (*jingqiang*, 京腔) in Beijing, and as "high-pitched tunes" (*gaoqiang*, 高腔). They originated in Yiyang, Jiangxi Province, and spread to Beijing during the Ming Dynasty, under Emperor Jiajing's reign (around 1720). From the beginning of the Qing Dynasty until the reigns of emperors Qianlong and Jiaqing, Yiyang tunes were quite popular on stages in Beijing, and having assimilated the folk music of the areas around Beijing, they gradually evolved into a system of tunes characteristic of Beijing, and were thus even better accepted by people from the capital, who called them "capital tunes." After the mid-period of Emperor Qianlong's reign, the *jingqiang*

An operatic stage

declined after the *bangzi* tunes from Shanxi and Shaanxi, the Anhui-style *pihuang* from Anhui and the Hubei-style *pihuang* from Hubei spread to Beijing.

Towards the end of Emperor Qianlong's reign (around the end of the 18th century), the *bangzi* tunes replaced *jingqiang* and became the

Peking opera body moves

major operatic tunes sung on Beijing stages. *Bangzi* tunes, or "Qin tunes" *(Qinqiang),* adopted the musical structure of "beat-and-tune" style *(ban qiang ti)*, which featured changes of musical metrics, and therefore were quite a departure from the fixed-melody style that had dominated China's operatic stage for several hundred years. At that time, people were bored with "capital tunes," and *bangzi* tunes charmed an increasing number of people thanks to their artistic freshness and vivacity. In the 45th year of Emperor Qianlong's reign (1780), Wei Changsheng, a performer of Qinqiang opera, went to Beijing from Sichuan and joined the Shuangqing Troupe to perform plays of Qinqiang opera, including *Falling Down the Stairs (gun lou,《滚楼》)* and *Entering the Lord's*

A Peking opera performance

Mansion with a Baby on the Back (*bei wa jin fu*,《背娃进府》). Wei Changsheng had such a handsome stage presence, along with a sweet voice, beautiful singing style and refined body postures, that his *Falling Down the Stairs* became an immediate success among his Beijing audience, and the Shuangqing Troupe thus became known as "No.1 in the capital." However, in the fiftieth year of Emperor Qianlong's reign (1785), the Qing government officially prohibited operatic troupes from performing Qinqiang opera in the capital and expelled Wei from Beijing; the development of Qinqiang in Beijing was thus negatively affected.

The Evolution of Peking Opera

Peking opera, as its name implies, must have taken shape and matured in the city of Beijing, but the predecessor of Peking opera was actually from Anhui, and Peking opera took shape after Anhui tunes assimilated the best artistic elements of other local operas and integrated with the local dialect. How, then, did a local opera from the south come to the capital city, and why did it stand out among all local operas and finally evolve into the best of all traditional Chinese operas? The story starts with some Anhui troupes coming to Beijing to participate in performances celebrating the 80th birthday of Emperor Qianlong.

The Anhui troupes popular in the areas around Anhui mainly sang the operatic tunes known as *chuiqiang* (吹腔), *gao bozi* (高拨子) and *erhuang* (二簧). Emperor Qianlong celebrated his 80th birthday in the year 1790, and officials all over the country prepared to celebrate this occasion, for which operatic performances were naturally indispensable. The celebration performances were extremely well organized and entertaining, with many stages set up along the streets within the city, and all operatic troupes vied to outdo each other in displays of splendor. What was not expected was that the troupe which stood out most of all in this grand event was the Sanqing Troupe of Anhui opera, recommended by Wulana (伍拉纳), the Minister of Salt of Zhejiang Province. The Emperor was very happy to watch the Anhui opera, which he had enjoyed during his past tours to the south of the Yangtze River; consequently, Wulana was generously rewarded, and the Sanqing Troupe became famous overnight.

The development of an art form, in China's feudal society, was impossible without the support of the imperial court and government, but in the case of a local opera, the most important factor was its popularity among ordinary people. After the performances to celebrate the Emperor's birthday, the Sanqing Troupe remained in Beijing and gave performances of Anhui opera to a larger audience. They were well received by the audience in the capital for their beautiful tunes and melodies, and henceforth gained a foothold there and gradually developed. Thereafter, its success attracted other Anhui opera troupes

Performance of the Peking opera play *The Best Scholar's Matchmaking*

Performance of the Peking opera play *The Best Scholar's Matchmaking*

to the capital, among which the most famous were the Sixi Troupe, the Hechun Troupe and the Chuntai Troupe. The four of them were later called the "Four Major Anhui Troupes" having come to the capital.

Having gained the favor of the Beijing audience, the artists of Anhui opera did not show any inclination to develop, but constantly assimilated the strengths of other operatic art forms, and integrated the best of them in terms of operatic tunes and performing art into Anhui opera. Besides, they also sought to reform the tunes and language in the plays to cater to the taste of local people in Beijing. Due to the rise of Anhui troupes in Beijing and the popularity of *erhuang* and *chuiqiang* tunes, performers of other opera, including Kunqu, *jingqiang* and Qinqiang, joined the Anhui troupes and thus enriched the operatic tunes and repertoire of Anhui operas. During the heyday of Anhui troupes in Beijing, artists of Han tunes (also called "Chu tunes") from Hubei also came to Beijing to give performances with the Anhui troupes, and the combination between the lingering beauty of the Han tunes and the mellow melodies of the Anhui tunes finally evolved into a new operatic form featuring even more diversified tunes and singing styles: Peking opera.

Thus we can see that Peking opera was formed by the integration of Anhui and Hubei tunes, and in its development, the tunes, metric beats, repertoire and rhymes of Han tunes became the "core" of Peking opera; as for the Anhui troupes, they became the "vehicle" through which all operatic tunes and forms integrated on the stage. Especially after performers of Han tunes joined the Anhui opera troupes, they collaborated with performers of Anhui opera to promote reform and innovation, which is why Peking opera acquired a distinctive style in terms of tunes, repertoire, stage language, performance and cast of performers. Over time, Peking opera — although born from Anhui troupes — came to combine the best traditions of multiple local operas including Anhui tunes, Han tunes, Kunqu, Qinqiang, *jingqiang* and folk music. It gradually matured, and finally became a Chinese cultural legacy enjoying great prestige in the world.

The Development of Peking Opera

In the 1840s, Peking opera took on a brand new look as a local opera, and it became a new fashion not only in the capital but all over the country. Wherever performers of Peking opera went, they caused a big stir among their local audience, and sometimes everyone in town would turn up to watch the performance. Later on, a number of well-known Peking opera performers went south to Shanghai, making Shanghai a Peking opera center on a par with Beijing. Peking opera in Shanghai gradually developed some unique characteristics, leading to a division between the "Beijing school" and the "Shanghai school." The Shanghai school started the very first reform campaign in the history of Peking

Photos of a Peking opera show

opera, making the operatic art more directly related to the social and historical circumstances of the country.

The development and thriving of Peking opera would have certainly been impossible without the favor and appreciation of the Qing Dynasty rulers. The feudal rulers were extremely strict with Peking opera troupes that performed before the imperial court. The performers had to comply with stringent requirements and overlook no detail in appearance, recitation, eye and facial expression, body movement and finger position, but also had to pay particular attention to the musical instruments, metric beats and all other aspects of performance. To a certain extent, this did promote the systemization and standardization

The "Four Great *Dan* Actors" of Peking opera

of Peking opera performances. The Qing rulers even established the Shengping Bureau (升平署) in order to administer the affairs related to Peking opera performances at the imperial court. Thereafter, Peking opera performances became regular events at the court. During this period, a large number of well-known Peking opera performers gathered at the imperial court, which became a favorable environment for artistic cooperation and exchange. Folk artists mainly performed for ordinary people, but sometimes they were also ordered to perform for the imperial court, and thus there were interactions and a mutual influence between the operatic performances designed for rulers and for commoners.

Shuangqing Troupe

Besides opera performances for the imperial court, the royal families, high officials and wealthy families also hired Peking opera troupes to perform in their private villas, which also had an influence on Peking opera at the time.

In any art form centered on performance, the performers themselves are bound to play a significant role in the development of this art form, and it is the performers who have given full expression to all artistic characteristics at every stage of the opera's development, so that at each stage, there are representative performers of Peking opera. Shen Rongpu (沈蓉圃), a folk painter from the late Qing Dynasty who was particularly skilled in portrait painting, once created a painting entitled *The Thirteen Best of the Tongguang Period* (《同光十三绝》), a portrait of well-known Peking opera artists during the period ranging from Emperor Tongguang's reign to Emperor Guangxu's reign. From the Tongguang period until the end of the Qing Dynasty, a number of outstanding performers in each line of business of Peking opera came to the fore. Famous actors of the first generation were Cheng Changgeng, Yu Sansheng and Zhang Erkui, followed by another trio of male roles: Tan Xinpei, Sun Juxian and Wang Guifen. One can see the inheritance and development of the traditions of the former trio by the latter trio of male roles, which are best embodied in the performance of Tan Xinpei. While carrying forward the tradition of the old generation of Peking opera artist, Tan brought the *lao sheng* role (representing a middle-aged or old man with a beard) to a great height of development. As the founder of "Tan School," Tan laid the foundation for the development of Peking opera for the following century, and thus he was honored as "King of Opera Performance." More importantly still, following in the footsteps of Cheng Changgeng and Yu Sansheng, Tan finally established the system of basic artistic styles of Peking opera and promoted the performance systemization of this operatic form, thus shaping the development pattern of Peking opera. Some well-known performers in other lines of business also contributed to the development of their respective roles and of the art of Peking opera.

The changes most characteristic of this development stage of Peking opera were the completion of its lines of business, and the development of a more refined performing art. It was not until the 1911 Xinhai Revolution that a complete system of role categories in Peking

Performance of the Peking opera play *The Fall of Gongsun Zidu*

opera took form, including *sheng* (male), *dan* (female), *jing* (painted face) and *chou* (clown) roles. Also at that time, the performing art, with its four main elements being singing, recitation, body movements and acrobatic fighting, no longer featured simplicity and vigor, like in Cheng Changgeng's time, but became more elegant and refined. Specifically, the singing tunes became more melodious, the body movements more stylish, the acrobatic fighting more clear-cut, and the focus of the performance was laid on characterization, and on depicting the psychological and emotional state of the characters. The singing style of Peking opera began to show its distinct characteristics during this time. The *pihuang* metric styles of Peking opera began to take shape, and many more flexible metric styles for singing tunes emerged. Tan Xinpei created the so-called "*er liu*" (literally "two-six," fast beats) and "shake beat," and another metric style, "*kuai san yan*" (快三眼, three fast weak beats), corresponding to a rhythm faster than the slow beats and slower than the original beats, so that the changes of metric styles became more flexible, as well as finer and smoother. The articulation of singing and recitation also showed some development: "*Hu Guang yin*" (the accents of Hubei and Guangdong areas) began to be adopted. Before Tan Xinpei, there were three schools of *lao sheng* roles performance: the Anhui school, the Hubei school and the Peking school, and articulation and intonation were not consistent between them. Tan Xinpei adopted a number of pronunciations and intonations from the accents of Hubei and Guangdong areas, and *Hu Guang yin* became the standard singing accent for *lao sheng* roles. Other aspects of stage performance art also showed great development, including the facial make-up, costumes, musical band, stage décor and props, and a large number of professional artists emerged, known for producing stage props and doing hair for Peking opera performers.

As Peking opera matured, the operation mechanism and system of performing troupes also tended to standardize, and many formerly implicit conventional rules began to be fixed in the form of explicit rules. In the past, the performing troupes adopted a "collective system" in which there was no distinction between performers and the other staff of the troupe, but thereafter, they began to adopt a new system in which well-reputed actors "shouldered the entire troupe," a system centered on the leading performers, in which other performers occupied a less prominent position. Representative plays performed by the leading actor of a troupe were more attractive to the audience, and in a theatrical show, this leading actor had to perform the last play so as to end the performance on a climax. At this time, leading actors of Peking opera troupes began to use their own string-instrument players and drum players. This new system burgeoned at the time of Cheng Changgeng, but it was formally established by Tan Xinpei. The system of income distribution was also modified. In the past, the actors received a fixed-

Mei Lanfang performing

Mei Lanfang

rate payment; when joining the performing troupe, they would agree with the boss on the amount, called *bao yin* (包银), or "contracted payment," which would remain unchanged for a whole year. Later, after some actors started to draw a large audience, they could require a certain share of income from the performances, which was called *xi fen* (戏份), literally "performance share." Now that the actors were paid a share on their own performances, it was no longer necessary for them to be bound to any performing troupe in particular; they could begin to sign contracts with the theatre, and gain a share from the theatre's income for their own performances, which was much more than *bao yin*. The emergence of these two systems concerning the operation of performing troupes and payment for performances promoted the development of Peking opera in

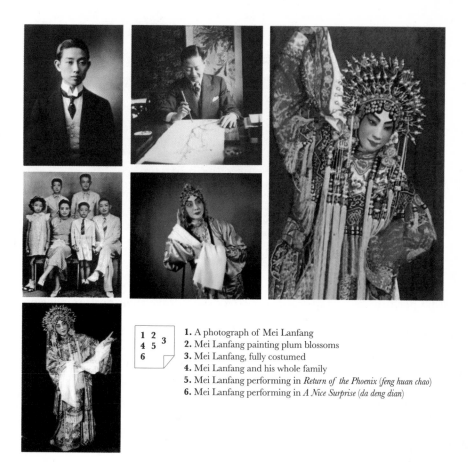

1. A photograph of Mei Lanfang
2. Mei Lanfang painting plum blossoms
3. Mei Lanfang, fully costumed
4. Mei Lanfang and his whole family
5. Mei Lanfang performing in *Return of the Phoenix* (*feng huan chao*)
6. Mei Lanfang performing in *A Nice Surprise* (*da deng dian*)

1 | 2 3
  | 4 5

1. Mei Lanfang performing in *Unexpected Reunion* (*qi shuang hui*)
2. Mei Lanfang visiting Hawaii
3. Mei Lanfang (*second from right*), the black American singer Paul Robeson (*first from left*) and others
4. Mei Lanfang wearing female character's head ornaments
5. Mei Lanfang visiting Japan

that performers had stronger incentives to improve their performance, in order to become popular among a larger audience. It was at that time that Mei Lanfang (1894-1961), a *dan* actor of Peking opera and Kunqu opera, the leading one of the "Four Great *Dan* Actors" and a well-known master of performing art, whose performance is recognized as "one of the three world contemporary systems of performing art" — the other two being Konstantin Stanislavski of Russia and Bertolt Brecht of Germany — made his debut in the circle of Peking opera, and his great fame further promoted the development of these systems.

As Peking opera gradually matured, artists collected the traditional

1. Mei Lanfang and Mei Weidong
2. Mei Lanfang putting on facial make-up
3. Mei Lanfang performing in *Chang'e Flying to the Moon* (*Chang'e ben yue*)

repertoire and made the plays more characteristic of Peking opera, and newly-created plays followed certain routines and conventions of this specific operatic form. The characterization of Peking opera plays put emphasis on the psychological and emotional state of the characters, and the performance was expected to seek "unity of form and spirit" — meaning that the performer's appearance should match the personality

1. Mei Lanfang and Mei Baojiu in a performance of *The Peony Pavilion (mu dan ting)*
2. Performance commemorating the 50th anniversary of the death of Mei Lanfang, October 2011
3. Mei Lanfang and Charlie Chaplin
4. Mei Baojiu and Ma Ying-jeou
5. Mei Lanfang and Guo Moruo

of the character he impersonated. And during this period of time, Peking opera performances were greatly enriched. Performance length varied between plays, one-act plays, playlets and serialized plays. Tan Xinpei collected and reformed the traditional repertoire of Peking opera, and he made the plays more artistically refined and inspiring. Based on his work, Mei Lanfang further reformed the repertoire and created many new plays.

A pioneer in the systematic promotion of the art of Peking opera to the outside world, Mr. Mei Lanfang traveled to Japan in 1919 at the invitation of the Tokyo Imperial Theatre, and performed Peking opera there for a month. He was so well received by the audience in Japan that

Mei Lanfang's painting "The Flower-Scattering Angel" (*tiannü san hua*)

Mei Lanfang's painting "The Nymph of the Luo River" (*luoshenfu*)

there was immediately a "Mei Lanfang fever" in the country, and later he revisited Japan twice in 1924 and 1956, respectively. The Japanese have been praising Mei Lanfang and the art of Peking opera ever since.

In 1930, Mei Lanfang went to the United States as the head of his theatrical company and put up performances in New York, Chicago, San Francisco and Los Angeles. This was the first time for Peking opera to be put on stage in a Western country, and Mei gained resounding success. Famous film stars, including Charlie Chaplin, were fascinated by Mei's performance. Besides, Mei's theatrical art was also admired by the US intelligentsia, so much so that both Pomona College and the University of Southern California awarded him honorary doctorate degrees in literature.

In 1935, Mei Lanfang visited the former Soviet Union with his theatrical company, and his performance caused a stir in the country. Sergei Eisenstein, a famous film director of the former Soviet Union, made a film of Mei's movements in his performance and of an excerpt of the play *The Rainbow Pass* (*hong ni guan*, 《虹霓关》). During his tour to Europe, Mei Lanfang exchanged his artistic ideas with a number of dramatists from the former Soviet Union and Europe, including Konstantin Stanislavski and Bertolt Brecht, and he not only gave extremely charming performances but also displayed the modesty and simplicity of Chinese artists to foreigners and won their appreciation and respect.

Artistic Characteristics of Peking Opera

The performance of Peking opera involves a whole set of rhythmic and stylized routines that are mutually binding and reinforcing, formulated over a long period of time through the stage practice of numerous generations of performers. Such a performance is an integration of various art forms, including literature, performing art, music, singing, musical ensemble as well as cosmetics and facial make-up. Peking opera adopted a rich variety of artistic means to create theatrical characters on the stage; the performers all have sets of strict rules to follow, and only the skillful mastery of these rules may enable them to give full expression to this operatic art. The performing art of Peking opera, as an outstanding representative of traditional Chinese opera, highlights the virtuality feature of the traditional Chinese theatre, which gives playwrights and performers considerable artistic freedom and greatly

Peking opera rehearsal

Mei Weidong (left), the author, with Mei Baojiu

Mei Baojiu and Fan Meiqiang , in *A Nice Surprise* (*da dengdian*)

enhances the expressiveness of performance within the confined physical space on stage. A Peking opera performance is elegant and stylish, and the tunes are sung with an excellent voice and the expression of deep emotions. Military plays themselves do not focus on violent actions, but are better performed in a graceful manner. The artistic characteristics of Peking opera can be summarized as follows.

Peking Opera Performance

Singing and Speaking Styles

Peking opera is a magical art form, in that the artistic effect of the performance is not realized through visual spectacle. During the decades since Peking opera took shape until its heyday, people actually went to the theatres and teahouses to "listen to the performance" instead of "watching the performance," which shows the crucial place of singing in this operatic form. When performing some roles that involve lots of singing, such as *qing yi* (starring female roles) and some painted-face roles (*tong chui hua lian*", 铜锤花脸), the performers often sing a very long passage immediately after they enter on the stage, thus attracting the audience with their appealing voice and singing style, and gaining loud applause. This is an important characteristic of Peking opera, and it is exactly why Peking opera has come to represent the quintessence of traditional Chinese culture, and is so widely known all over the world.

The music structure of Peking opera follows a "beat-and-tune style" (*ban qiang ti*), as part of the *pihuang* (皮簧) tune system, and featuring the combination of various metric types. While Peking opera tunes follow strict rules, they also show great flexibility. As for the lyrics, they mainly consist of seven-character or ten-character couplets.

Peking opera is also known as "*pihuang* opera" (皮簧戏) because it evolved from two basic tunes, *xipi* and *erhuang*. It is believed that *xipi* was taken from Hubei opera, which itself was formed under the influence of Shaanxi opera (Qinqiang), and that *erhuang* came from Anhui opera. *Xipi* tunes are generally fresh, clear and melodic, used to express the happiness or excitement of characters, while *erhuang* tunes are stable and strong, and generally used to express a meditative or melancholy mood. Each set of tunes includes a wealth of variations, and thus does not really fit the above definition. The timing of a melody is indicated by *ban* and *yan*. *Ban* is the accented or strong beat while *yan* is the unaccented or weak beat. A piece of *xipi* tune starts with the weak beat and does not feature clear-cut rhythmic contours, which is why *xipi* tunes are free-flowing; as to the *erhuang* tune, it starts with a strong beat, and its strong-weak rhythm is quite distinct, which is why *erhuang* tunes are strong and powerful.

Apart from the aforementioned *xipi* and *erhuang* tunes, in the

Mei Baojiu with some Peking opera performers

Mei Baojiu with some Peking opera performers

A Peking opera band

course of its development, Peking opera also assimilated tunes from other operas — such as Kunqu opera, Yiyang tunes and *bangzi* tunes — and from folk music, and these are termed "other tunes" [than *xipi* and *erhuang*]. After being assimilated into Peking opera, these tunes began to merge with *xipi* and *erhuang*, and became an integral part of Peking opera. The rhythm of Peking opera tunes is expressed as "metric types" (*ban shi*, 板式). Its musical structure is, as mentioned above, "beat-and-tune style," which is also called "changing metric-type style" (*ban shi bian hua ti*, 板式变化体). As this name implies, the operatic effect of Peking opera is created by varying combinations of various tunes and metric types.

In Peking opera circles, there is a popular saying: "A little recitation is as good as much singing," and this denotes the importance of recitation in the operatic performance. There are two kinds of recitation in Peking opera: lines spoken in Beijing dialect, called *jing bai* (京白), and rhymed lines, called *yun bai* (韵白). *Jing bai*, spoken in the local dialect, is clear, easy to understand, witty and true to life. *Yun bai*, on the other hand, is a stage language full of artistic refinement, an embellished speaking style more melodically aesthetic. The recitation of *yun bai* resembles singing, and its melodic, rhymed and rhythmic tones are best used to express the complex emotions of characters, making it a means of expression better suited to show the characters' psychological and emotional state.

As a quintessence of traditional Chinese opera, apart from its singing and speaking style, the artistic charm of Peking opera also lies in its beautiful music. Besides the aforementioned metric types and tunes, an important part of the music is fixed melodies. These fixed melodies were originally used by artists raised in the traditions of other Chinese operas to compose rhymed lyrics to their tunes; later, Peking opera artists selected a few of the best, and integrated them into the music of this particular operatic form. There is a rich variety of fixed melodies in Peking opera, which are extremely expressive not only in creating an atmosphere suitable for dramatic development, but in portraying the dramatic characters in the plays. There are types of fixed melodies to fit all kinds of scenes, contexts, and occasions, and the characters' every

Peking opera band accompaniment

physical and psychological experience. The fixed melodies have different names according to the musical instruments that are used, including "*hun ban* melodies" (混板牌子) accompanied by gongs and drums, "*qing ban* melodies" (清板牌子) accompanied by string instruments, "*cu chui da* melodies" (粗吹打乐) with the *suona* as the major instrument of musical accompaniment, and "*xi chui da* melodies" (细吹打乐) with bamboo flute as the major instrument of musical accompaniment.

Movements and Postures

Body movements and postures, as part of the Peking opera performance, originate from the artistic processing of everyday movements, so that all postures and movements of performers on

Mei Baojiu

the stage, including hand movements, footwork and the use of eye expressions, are stylized and exaggerated to an extreme, and performers must be trained rigorously from a young age and follow strict rules in their performance. An example of this is the rule of "hands pointing to a direction, and the eyes following the hands to that direction" (以眼领手, 以手引眼). This refers to the fact that regardless of the action performed, the performer's eye expressions should be perfectly coordinated with his/ her hand gestures and body movements, while at the same time, his/her eye expression should provide indications about the movements about to follow. For instance, if the performer needs to point with his finger at somebody or something to the front right side of the stage, he/she should first raise his finger to his breast, move his finger in a small arc over to his left shoulder, thereby pointing his finger to the left behind him, and then move his finger downward in a large arc, then up to the object to the front right side; and while performing this whole set of hand movements, his/her eyes should follow his hand closely, and move along with it. Thus we can see that even for such a simple hand movement, a series of rules exist in order to exaggerate it and make it larger than life. The purpose of this is to make each and every move clearer, more vivid and beautiful in the eyes of the audience. The performing art of Peking opera therefore seeks a similarity between art and life in spirit, and understanding this exaggeration in Peking opera may help one better understand this performing art, and find the realness of life within it.

The characteristics of posture and body movements in the performance of Peking opera can be summarized as follows:

Dance-like stage movements, generally speaking, involve exaggerating and beautifying body movements based on an understanding of our everyday movements, so as to make them look like dancing. Such is the *pao yuan chang* (跑圆场, literally "running around the center of a stage to indicate that the character is on a journey") move of *dan* roles, for example, which takes place in dramatic scenes. In order to imitate the running pace of his female character, the *dan* actor takes small and mincing steps so that feet movements are invisible to the audience. If the actor has a good mastery of related skills, he should appear to be gliding over the stage, with his upper limbs remaining still. In real life, whenever running fast, one tends to run straight ahead; within the confined space on stage, however, the actor must run around the center of the stage, and therefore possess solid *pao yuan chang* skills, in order to convey the relative aesthetic effect to the audience.

There are two kinds of dance-like movements in Peking opera. One involves imitating everyday life movements, rather simple and easy to perform, such as eating, drinking, writing, threading and sewing, and opening doors. These movements, however, are not acted out in the form of a dance, but have the only aim of contributing to the dramatic

Peking opera acrobatic fighting scene

Typical Peking opera moves

development of the play, and of expressing the characters' state of mind. The other kind of dance-like movements involve largely exaggerated and beautified movements, and as embellished movements, they are highly conventionalized, with a set of standards to be followed. In the case of horse riding, for example, the *ma tang zi* (马趟子, literally "a horse-riding trip") move involves performing with a whip as the only prop. Since waving a whip is a typical horse-riding move, when doing so an actor can guarantee the audience immediately understands that he is now riding a horse, and consciously integrates this move with the current dramatic context. In the Peking opera play *The Battle of Wancheng* (*zhan wan cheng*,《战宛城》) there is a scene entitled "Riding on the Young Crop" (*ma ta qing miao*, "马踏青苗"), in which the body movements, facial expressions and hand gestures of whip waving not only represent the horse and its rider, but also indicate the character Cao Cao's state of mind, flustered and irritated. This is a typical example of the characteristics of body movements in Peking opera, from which we can see that a skillful performance of conventionalized movements in Peking opera (as well as in all traditional Chinese operas) may create the desired artistic effect.

Qi ba ("[military officers] adjusting a helmet on their armor upon entering the stage", 起霸) is another example of this. This series of conventionalized movements originated in the dancing of the character Xiang Yu (called *Chu Ba Wang*, "the Conqueror of Chu") as he prepared for war, in the Ming Dynasty romance play *A Tale of One Thousand Taels of Gold* (*qian jin ji*,《千金记》). Later, this series of dancing movements became a norm, and were conventionalized as moves to be performed by all kinds of military officer characters in Peking opera before going into battle. Actually, *qi ba*, as a series of exaggerated conventionalized movements, has a more important function — namely, to convey to the audience the high fighting spirit of military characters in the play.

Acrobatic fighting is an important part of a Peking opera performance, as it is involved in the war and fighting action represented on stage. Peking opera acrobatic fighting moves find their root in Chinese martial arts, from which generations of artists extracted typical fighting movements, integrated elements of Chinese acrobatics and dancing, thus forming the acrobatic fighting moves characteristic of traditional Chinese operas, which are endowed with great aesthetic taste and value. These acrobatic fighting movements not only imitate real-life fighting, but also contribute to dramatic development, context, atmosphere, and to establish the personality traits of all characters. Hence there is the Peking opera rule of *"wu xi wen chang"* (武戏文唱), meaning that military plays must not feature violent actions, and are best performed in a graceful manner. There are many fighting movements and methods to represent a warlike atmosphere on the stage, and all these movements are dance-like and must be enacted with performing skills. When characters carry out all kinds of acrobatic fighting movements on stage in a swift and skillful manner, to the fast-paced beats of gongs and drums, the audience immediately feels the fiery atmosphere of war. Actors of military plays therefore receive rigorous training over those basic acrobatic movements from a very young age.

Another kind of skills are called *juehuo'er* (绝活儿), meaning feats or stunts. In Peking opera, there was once a feat called *qiaogong* (跷功, stilt skills),

Typical Peking opera moves

Peking opera acrobatic fighting scenes

which portrayed steps made by a woman with bound feet. At the time, all Peking opera performers were big-footed men. Someone invented the method of having a male actor's feet supported by wooden sticks to perform such steps. An actor needed to practice two to three years to master this technique. Fans are also frequently used in Peking opera. In *Hong Niang the Maidservant* (*hong niang*, 《红娘》), the maid uses a round fan to catch butterflies. In other plays, female characters usually use folding fans. As performances involving fans grew in number, there came into being the so-called "fan skills," which have become basic acting skills in Peking opera. Fans are used for different purposes: for cooling oneself, but also to help convey a certain meaning, such as emphasizing what the user is saying or indicating a distance. There are other kinds of feats in Peking opera, such as "handkerchief skills," "beard skills," "hair-throwing skills" and "chair skills." They all are extremely difficult to learn, and are usually used to represent a special context in the dramatic development.

Artistic Features of Peking Opera

In his book *History and Criticism of Chinese Drama* (《戏曲考源》) written in 1902, renowned Chinese scholar and theatrical theorist Wang Guowei (王国维, 1877-1927) defined traditional Chinese *xiqu* as

Peking opera performance

Wang Guowei (1877-1927), a renowned Chinese scholar and theatrical theorist

"an interpretation of stories in the form of songs and dances."[1] Being an integration of various artistic elements, a Peking opera performance combines singing, musical composition, dancing, fine arts, literature, facial make-up, lighting, costumes and acrobatic skills. It is said to be "dancing whenever there is movement, and singing whenever there is sound," which differentiates it from Western opera, ballet or drama, as the latter can reach completion as a single form, be it singing, dancing, or the dramatic dialogue. The reason for this is that throughout its hundreds of years of development, Peking opera assimilated multiple artistic forms from folk singing and dancing, burlesque and the singing style of other operas, integrating songs, dances, poetry and fine arts into a harmonious

---

1" 戏曲者，谓以歌舞演故事也。"

Peking opera dance move

whole, which therefore is "an interpretation of stories in the form of songs and dances."

On the Peking opera stage, all details extracted from everyday life are refined, standardized, exaggerated, beautified and adorned, thus forming the artistic features that are unique to this art form. Of these features, the conventional rules and the expressivity achieved by virtuality are best suited to represent the artistic charms of Peking opera, and the integration of these two elements has made Peking opera the culmination

Peking opera performance

of performing art shown on the Chinese operatic stage, as well as an outstanding tribute to the art of the traditional Chinese opera.

Conventional rules refer to the means of artistic expression that involve the refining, standardizing and beautifying of real-life movements according to certain standards, followed by the formation of a whole set of conventions to be followed by performers. Performance aside, there are conventions regulating the use of costumes, facial make-up, role categories, metric types of music and even recitation. The conventions in Peking opera can be seen as a mature means of artistic expression, for they contain extremely rich and flexible combinations of various rules. In addition, these conventions were established in the process of a hundred years of practice, successively compiled by many performers, and passed down from generation to generation. While they are relatively fixed rules, breaking with accepted routines is allowed, which gives them great flexibility. Consider a character's self-introduction at the opening of a play, for instance. The entrance of Zhuge Liang in *The Loss of Jieting Fort* (*shi jie ting*, 《失街亭》) and that of Emperor Xian of the Han Dynasty in *The Xiaoyao Ferry* (*xiao yao jin*, 《逍遥津》) depict radically different personalities and plots. Zhuge Liang makes a "tiger-head introduction" (*hu tou yin zi*, 虎头引子) or "double introduction" (*shuang yin zi*, 双引子) to assert his military bearing and ambition to defeat his enemies in Qishan; but as Emperor Xian pronounces his opening words, on the other hand, he sees Cao Cao coming to the court combatively and holding a sword, and he is so frightened that he retreats to his seat without even completing his introduction — an evidence of the emperor's cowardice and of Cao Cao's arrogance and domineering attitude. Thus we can see that the use of conventional rules can change along with the dramatic plot, and in this sense, they are relatively flexible. On another level, each role category has its own strict rules to follow in terms of facial make-up, singing and speaking styles. Regarding hand movements, for example, each role category may only perform them in a certain way: *lao sheng* actors should raise their hands to their eyebrows, *dan* actors to their chests, "painted-face" actors over their heads, *xiao sheng* actors to their shoulders and *wu chou* (clowns with martial arts skills) actors to their abdomens. These rules actually apply to all body movements in Peking opera.

Virtuality can be defined as follows: the opera background changes with the performance of the actors, who must guide the audience through the dramatic scenes by means of their acting and of their empathy with their characters, which can be regarded as a kind of artistic impressionism. For example, a Peking opera stage seldom contains more than a table and two chairs, hence the audience has no indication whatsoever as to what these props represent before the play starts; indeed, only through the actors' performance can one comprehend the time, place and surrounding environment of the play, and begin to embark on a dramatic adventure with the actors. How, then, can the Chinese audience accept and appreciate this dramatic form? The reason lies in the emphasis that is placed on "imagery" in traditional Chinese culture, which seeks for "similarity in spirit." The beauty of virtuality in Peking opera is that thanks to the emptiness of the stage, spectators can give

Peking opera performance

full play to their imagination: impressionism wins over realism. When an official is seen to be sitting majestically behind the table, the scene is understood to take place in a solemn government office; but when people are drinking and playing to some jolly music, the setting is a banquet hall. Even the complete absence of any prop on stage does not hinder the actors from providing the audience with indications about the scene. For instance, when two fully-armored generals start to wield their weapons to the fierce sound of gongs and drums, the scene obviously takes place in a battlefield, and when two girls are frolicking and admiring flowers, they

Peking opera performance

can only be in a blossoming garden. In Peking opera, "the props appear through the actors' performance," and the dramatic scenes are entirely born from this performance, as well as the accompanying costumes and music. However, the virtuality of Peking opera is not ungrounded, but is based on people's shared experience and understanding of their everyday life. It functions as a spiritual interaction between the actors and the audience, and through the shared imagination of both.

The virtuality of Peking opera also helps it break through the spatiotemporal confines of the stage. The Western drama, based on ancient Greek dramatic theories, emphasizes the so-called "three unities" — namely the unity of action, which means a play should have one main action, with no or few subplots; the unity of place, according to which a play should cover a single physical space and should not attempt to compress geography, nor should the stage represent more than one place; and the unity of time, meaning the action in a play should take place over no more than 24 hours.[①] Peking opera completely differs from Western drama in this regard. In Peking opera, it is said that "within the tiny space of the stage, everything is so close and yet so far in terms of both time and space."[②] For example, when actors of Peking opera wish to represent a powerful military troop marching from one place to another, no matter how far apart these two places are from each other, the actors just need to walk about in circles on the stage for the audience to know they are traveling all the way to their destination. The key point here is that the artists and the spectators of Peking opera have an unspoken consensus that marching is actually a change of geographical location, so that there is no need to represent the distance in a precise way. There are other special means of representation in Peking opera to break through the spatial confines of the stage, so that two events happening at the same

---

① http://en.wikipedia.org/wiki/Classical_unities.
② "舞台方寸地，咫尺见天涯。"

time in two different places can be represented on the stage at the same time, which may have an effect like that of a split screen shot in a film. The fact that this modern means of artistic representation was used so skillfully in such an ancient operatic form as Peking opera may be one of the key reasons explaining why Peking opera has flourished over time, and still remains extremely charming to audiences worlwide.

These artistic features of Peking opera allow the audience plenty of space for imagination, and make the opera an art form able to record and present the country's colorful social life and rich historical and cultural traditions. This is the reason Peking opera is such an outstanding local opera with lasting and exuberant vitality.

Role Categories of Peking Opera

Sheng Roles

Peking Opera features "role categorization." In accordance with gender and disposition, characters are divided into four basic roles: *sheng* (male roles), *dan* (female roles), *jing* (characters with a painted face) and *chou* (clown). Each role category comes with its own subdivisions.

The *sheng* is a grown-up male, and it can be further divided into four subdivisions. The *lao sheng* is a middle-aged or old man with a

Lao sheng character

Hong sheng character

beard; it can specialize in singing, or in martial arts. The *lao sheng* is the most common male role in Peking opera. Cheng Changgeng and Tan Xinpei, regarded as the founders of Peking opera, were both *lao sheng* actors. The *wu sheng*, or "man with martial arts skills," is the second subdivision. A *wu sheng* actor can specialize in long weapons or short weapons. The long-weapon *wu sheng* wears armor, looks dignified and has moderate singing and recitation skills, whereas the short-weapon *wu sheng* wears short clothes and is swift in action. The *xiao sheng*, third subdivision under the line of *sheng*, plays the role of young handsome men, most of whom are young scholars. This role is frequently portrayed

Xiao sheng character

Wu sheng character

Performance of the Peking opera play *The Best Scholar's Matchmaking*

in love stories. The *xiao sheng* can be further classified as a gauze-hat *sheng* (a court official), a fan *xiao sheng* (a scholar using a fan), a pheasant-feather fan *sheng* (a handsome young man) or a poor *sheng* (a scholar failing to become an official). The pheasant-feather fan *sheng*, though not belonging to the subdivision of *wu sheng*, are usually young and handsome characters both well-educated and trained in military exercises, such as Zhou Yu in *The Battle of Wits* (*qun ying hui*,《群英会》) and *Back to Jingzhou* (*hui jing zhou*,《回荆州》) or Yang Zongbao in *The Muke Stronghold* (*mu ke zhai*,《穆柯寨》). Another subdivision in the business line of *sheng* is that of *hong sheng*. This is a red-faced character (*hong* means red), usually corresponding to either of two prototypical historical figures: Guan Yu and Zhao Kuangyin.

Owing to the uniqueness of Peking opera, the role of *xiao sheng* had long been relatively unimportant. While many plays give prominence to *lao sheng* characters and *dan* (female) roles, *xiao sheng* remains relatively obscure. In the history of Peking opera, there are few well-known actors specializing in *xiao sheng* roles. Earlier acclaimed *xiao sheng* actors were Cheng Jixian (1874-1944), Jiang Miaoxiang (1890-1972) and Jin Zhongren (1886-1950). Later renowned performers were Yu Zhenfei (1902-1993) and Ye Shenglan (1914-1978). Among *xiao sheng* performers, the only one to have been a leading actor in Peking opera plays was Ye Shenglan, who was first in the history of Peking opera to have turned *xiao sheng* roles into major performance protagonists. In the *xiao sheng* business line, Ye Shenglan notably played the parts of Zhou Yu and Luo Cheng in the eponymous plays *Zhou Yu* (《周瑜》) and *Luo Cheng* (《罗成》).

This is quite different from Western drama, in which the young hero is often very important and is played by highly acclaimed actors. In performance, the *xiao sheng*'s most striking feature is a singing and speaking style which combines chest voice and falsetto. His falsetto is relatively high-pitched and fine, making the role distinctively different

Qing yi character

Hua dan character

Dao ma dan (*dan* character riding a horse with a sword in hand)

Lao dan character

from that of *lao sheng*. On the other hand, *xiao sheng*'s falsetto should be strong enough to differ from that of *dan* roles. It is not easy to master the fine-tuning nuances of a *xiao sheng*'s singing style, which is why few actors excelled at playing in this line of business.

Dan Roles

The *dan* actors play various types of female roles, corresponding to a wide range of social status, ages and personalities. *Dan* roles can be further classified as *qing yi* (青衣), *hua dan* (花旦), *hua shan* (花衫), *wu dan* (武旦) and *lao dan* (老旦).

The *qing yi*, also called *zheng dan*, plays the part of young or middle-aged female characters who are traditionally demure and dignified, such as understanding wives, loving mothers, and chaste widows. Most *qing yi* (also known as *qing shan*) actors wear black garments, which explains this role's denomination — meaning "black garment."

The *hua dan* plays lively and cheerful young female characters with a witty mind and graceful motions; they are usually girls of ordinary family background, or of vivacious disposition. Most *hua dan* actors wear short costumes like short gowns, short trousers, short coats and short skirts, all in bright colors.

The *hua shan* is a role that combines the characteristics of *qing yi* and *hua dan* roles. It was invented by Wang Yaoqing, who was not only a famous actor of Peking opera, but also a good judge of talent, and many famous performing artists we know today, including the "Four Great *Dan* Actors," Mei Lanfang, Cheng Yanqiu, Shang Xiaoyun and Xun Huisheng, learned to perform with him or asked him for advice. Seeking to strengthen the artistic expressiveness of *dan* roles, Wang Yaoqing integrated the different features of *qing yi*, *hua dan* and even *wu dan*, created a new subdivision of *dan* roles that paid equal attention to singing, recitation, acting and acrobatic fighting, and gave it the name *hua shan*, implying that it is an integration of **hua** *dan* and *qing* **shan** (*qing yi*).

Wu dan actors play the part of female characters that are skilled at martial arts. The *wu dan* can likewise be divided into two types: *wu dan* in short costumes, who usually do not ride horses, and *wu dan* in long garments, helmets and armor, who usually ride a horse. Since the character often held a short sword in her hand, a *wu dan* role in long garment could also be called *dao ma dan* (刀马旦, the *dan* character riding a horse and with a sword in hand).

Lao dan actors play the part of old female characters.

As mentioned above, during the earlier development of Peking opera the leading roles were all *lao sheng* roles, that is to say mature male characters with a prominent social status. In the feudal society, Peking opera itself was an ideological instrument. Loyal court officials and generals were regarded as the mainstay of society in all dynastic periods. Their character and moral standards represented the mainstream values of society. It was only in the 1920s that the *dan* roles played by Mei Lanfang gained great popularity; Peking opera then underwent a major shift, from an emphasis on moral education to an emphasis on aesthetic appreciation. Female characters became as important as their male counterparts in Peking opera.

Jing Roles

The *jing*, also called *hua lian* (characters with exaggerated facial

Zheng jing character

make-up, 花脸), are male roles with distinct personalities, dispositions and appearances. These characters display a great variety in their personalities: upright and honest, resolute and brave, rude and rash, cunning and deceitful, or even cruel and outrageous; they can also be of all ages and from all social backgrounds. Certain colors of paint are used to distinguish between different personalities, and to express the playwrights' (and the audience's) judgment about the characters themselves. The singing and speaking style of *jing* roles is strong and powerful, and their facial expressions and body movements embody the manliness and arrogance of male characters. *Jing* roles can be further

Fu jing character

divided into three subcategories, *zheng jing* (正净), *fu jing* (副净) and *wu jing* (武净).

The *zheng jing*, also called *da hua lian* (大花脸, first-rank *hua lian*), usually specializes in singing, and is often referred to as "singing *hua lian*." Speaking of the tunes and recitation of Peking opera, above, we mentioned the term "*tong chui hua lian*" (铜锤花脸, "*tong chui*" meaning "bronze hammer"), which is a subtype of singing *hua lian*. In the play *Entering the Palace Twice* (er jin gong, 《二进宫》), the painted-face character Xu Yanzhao is a singing *hua lian*. Stepping onto the stage with a bronze hammer in hand, this character has almost no

Peking opera performance

body movement, but simply stands there and sings his lines, which is why people use the term "*tong chui*" while referring to the *zheng jing*, or the singing *hua lian*. Another subtype of singing *hua lian* is the *hei tou* (黑头, "black type"), which originated in Peking opera plays featuring Bao Zheng — a well-known historical figure living in the Song Dynasty, and the archetype of the impartial official who always protects ordinary people's rights and interests — such as *Beating the Dragon Robe* (*da long pao*,《打龙袍》), *Judge Bao and His Sister-in-Law* (*chi sang zhen*,《赤桑镇》), or *The Case of the Ungrateful Husband's Execution* (*zha mei an*,《铡美案》). Because the face of the Bao Zheng character in these plays is always painted black ("*hei tou*" means "black head"), and since this character sings a lot in these plays, people use the term *hei tou* to refer to singing *hua lian*.

The *fu jing* includes the *jia zi hua lian* (架子花脸, minor painted face roles) and the *er hua lian* (二花脸, second-rank *hua lian*). The actors playing *jia zi hua lian* roles must be skilled in body movements, recitation and performance. The acting style of the *er hua lian* is similar to that of clowns. Sometimes, *fu jing* actors also play the part of humorous or cunning characters.

Wu jing roles are also called *wu er hua* (武二花) or *shuai da hua lian* (摔打花脸, literally "beating painted-face"). They focus much more on acrobatic fighting than on singing or recitation. At an earlier stage, some *wu jing* roles also emphasized body postures, performance and recitation, but later on, these parts were gradually played by *wu sheng* actors; similarly, some *wu jing* roles involving much acrobatic fighting were gradually played by *jia zi hua lian* actors. As a result, there are fewer parts in the line of *wu jing* in Peking opera plays today. The only three *wu jing* characters left are the black-faced tiger in *At the White Beach* (*bai shui tan*,《白水滩》), Yu Hong in *The Bamboo Grove Ruse* (*zhu lin ji*,《竹林计》) and Hei Fengli in *Thrusting Aside Rolling Carts* (*tiao hua che*,《挑滑车》).

Chou Roles

The *Chou*, or clown, is also called *xiao hua lian* (小花脸, little painted-face roles) or *san hua lian* (三花脸, third-rank *hua lian*). This

Civilian clown (*wen chou*) character   Military clown (*wu chou*) character

is a lower rank among the role categories of Peking opera. *Chou* roles can be evil characters or kind figures, and while *chou* actors usually impersonate insidious, cunning and selfish characters, they may also play upright people with sharp wits and good humor. In traditional Peking opera, the parts of people with lower social status, such as fishermen and messengers, were usually played by *chou* actors, and were generally of a humorous nature. *Chou* roles can be divided into "civilian clowns" (*wen chou*, 文丑) and "clowns with martial arts skills" (*wu chou*, 武丑).

Role categorization is actually a generalization of various types of people in our everyday life. Among a Peking opera audience, as with all

other traditional Chinese operas, when one is familiar with the role categories, he or she can gain a better knowledge and understanding of the characters on the stage by taking note of their cosmetic style, costumes, performance and singing tunes. In this way, he or she may pay more attention to details pertaining to the singing, speaking and performing style of the individual actors, and seek an in-depth understanding of the characters — which is the best way for anyone to appreciate the performing art of Peking opera.

The Auspicious Dragon and Phoenix

Other Artistic Features of Peking Opera

Facial Make-up and *Lian Pu*

As an operatic form with distinctive characteristics regarding conventionalizing and virtuality, Peking opera not only differs from Western-style dramatic art in terms of performance, singing style, recitation and body movements, but has its unique and refined traditions in terms of cosmetics, costumes, props, musical accompaniment and stage art.

Facial Make-up

Peking opera facial make-up is extremely exaggerated and conventionalized. The faces of the actors are painted in extremely bright and colorful ways, and colors are combined to form sharp contrasts. The facial make-up used by characters in Peking opera is consistent with the aesthetic standards of traditional Chinese culture, notably through the color archetypes involved. Red, white and black are three major colors, used in grand events or ceremonies in the ancient Chinese society, and traditionally, each of these colors corresponds to certain fixed impressions in people's minds. White stands for purity, and it forms a sharp contrast with the color black, while red is the bright color that has the most intriguing visual effect. An often-cited example of this is the scene "The Oath of Brotherhood in the Peach Garden" from the historical novel

Romance of the Three Kingdoms(san guo yan yi,《三国演义》), in which Liu Bei, Zhang Fei and Guan Yu wear exactly these three colors, respectively. The facial make-up of both *sheng* and *dan* roles highlights these three major colors: their skin, teeth and the white of their eyes are painted very white, their eyebrows, eyelashes and hair the darkest black, and

A Peking opera mask

their lips and faces gorgeously red, so that the actors may display utmost clarity of facial contour and leave a deep impression on the audience. Based on this principle, the age of characters and even their personalities and dispositions may sometimes be represented through specific combinations of facial make-up colors.

Lian Pu

Color patterns painted on the faces of operatic characters are called *lian pu* (脸谱, "facial make-up types"), and represent a special feature of Peking opera based on real life. Mr. Weng Ouhong, a well-known Chinese theatrical theorist, once stated that *lian pu* in Peking opera has five functions. The first is descriptive, meaning the facial make-up types inform the audience about the skin color and facial contours of certain

Peking opera masks

characters. The second is symbolic, meaning the colors are symbolic of the personalities of different characters. The third is judgmental, meaning the facial make-up types indicate the moral integrity of the characters. The fourth is indicative, in the sense that they further point to the characters' specific personality traits. And the last is pictographic,

Putting on facial make-up before a Peking opera performance

meaning sometimes, especially in plays containing supernatural elements, animal images may be painted on certain characters, mostly to indicate they are ghosts and goblins.

A facial make-up type points to the personality of a particular character type. A red face indicates uprightness and loyalty, a black face a rough and forthright character, a blue face bravery and pride, a white face treachery and cunning, and a face with a white patch a fawning and base character. As a mark of kinship, father and son may have faces of the same color with similar patterns. A face with a "dignified pattern" is that of a loyal official or loving son, a blue-and-green face that of an outlawed hero, a face with kidney-shaped eyes and wooden-club-shaped eyebrows that of a monk, a face with sharp eye corners and a small mouth that of a court eunuch, and a face with a white patch that of a minor character.

When actors with full make-up come onto the stage, the audience may have the impression that all these kinds of facial make-up resemble masks painted on the actors' faces. Therefore *lian pu* patterns do have the symbolic function of masks, but they are more real and lively, and not as rigid as real masks. Since the *lian pu* in Peking opera are certain types of colors painted on the actors' faces in certain shapes, they can move along with the actors' facial expressions, and thus represent the emotional states of the characters.

Peking Opera Costumes

Peking opera costumes are called *xingtou* (行头) or, more popularly, *xifu* (戏服), and they are widely different from the clothes worn by people in modern society. The origins of Peking opera costumes can be traced back to the mid-14th century, when operatic precursors first began experimenting with large ornate articles of clothing. The costumes of Peking opera are quite complex, but they are designed following certain conventions, and may be used by actors in different plays. This is made possible because the basic designs of Peking opera costumes were established according to the clothes worn by people in the Ming Dynasty, with consideration of certain Song and Yuan dynasties garments, and costume designers gradually carried out such a vast amount of reworking over them that they have evolved into shapes that are specific to no historical period in particular. However, Peking opera costumes remain specific to the social status and position — among other particularities

Peking opera costumes

Peking opera hats

— of certain characters, for which a set of strict rules must be followed; according to a well-known saying among Peking opera performers, "better wear ragged clothes than wrong costumes." A performer should know what costume to wear when playing a certain role, since wearing the wrong costume would be unacceptable to the audience. As most Peking opera plays recount historical stories, costume shapes are fixed and categorized. Generally speaking, theatrical costumes are divided into five categories: *mang* (蟒,the ceremonial robe embroidered with patterns of a four-toed dragon and sea-waves worn by emperors or high-rank officials), *kao* (靠, a warrior's suit of armor), *zhe* (褶, a lined coat), *pei* (帔, a mantle worn by male or female roles) and *yi* (衣, other costumes). Whoever wears a yellow robe with python patterns is an emperor, and whoever wears a blue gown

1 2 3

1. *Mang* (ceremonial robe embroidered with patterns of a four-toed dragon and sea-waves, worn by emperors or high-rank officials)
2. A character wearing platform boots (*hou di xue*)
3. A Peking opera crown

and a black hat is a scholar. A character's identity is thus easily known from what he wears.

In Peking opera, costumes must enable the audience to distinguish a character's sex and status at first glance. In terms of symbolism, these costumes reflect each character's position in the social hierarchy: official or simple citizen, of noble or humble birth, civilian or military functions. By means of this subtle codification, Peking opera costumes often express sharp distinctions between good and evil or, preferably, loyal and wicked characters. Oblong wings (*chi zi*, 翅子) attached to a gauze hat

1. Colored shoes, part of a Peking opera costume
2. Platform boots (*hou di xue*)
3. Peking opera hat

1 2 3

indicate a loyal official. In contrast, a corrupt official is made to wear a gauze hat with rhomboidal wings. Baldrics, though apparently of little or no account compared to such important items as crowns and robes, may nevertheless function to bring about more dramatic effects on the stage. For instance, the wings attached to a hat, the plumes (*ling zi*, 翎子) pinned to a helmet and the cascading sleeves (*shui xiu*, 水袖) sewn to a garment accentuate movement even though they have little practical use.

In the early days, opera costumes were mainly made of wool or coarse cloth; later, satin, crepe and silk were used, decorated with various meticulously embroidered patterns. The making of opera costumes is a special and unique craft. The costume box first appeared in the Ming Dynasty (1368-1644), and was greatly improved during the Qing Dynasty

(1644-1911).

There are 20 major kinds of costumes, including, as mentioned above, ceremonial robes, informal robes and armor for soldiers. Ten colors are used in total, but half of all costumes display only the "five primary colors" (*shang wu se*, 上五色), namely red, green, yellow, white and black, in contrast to the other group of colors, which includes pink, blue, purple, pale-brown and pale-blue, all of which are labeled secondary colors (*xia wu se*, 下五色).

Many details are to be taken into account regarding costumes. For example, while the *mang* is the costume generally worn by both the emperor and nobles, there are subtle variations between them. For instance, the emperor's *mang* bears an open-mouthed dragon, while the dragon on the *mang* worn by ministers and generals has its mouth closed. The dragons on the costume of civil officials are gentle and quiet, while those on the costume of martial officials are bold and mighty. There are also clear distinctions in the use of colors. For example, a red *mang* stands for majesty and nobleness; a green *mang* indicates might and boldness; a white *mang* is worn by handsome young people, and a black *mang* is reserved for upright and loyal characters. There are also simplified *mang,* and *mang* specifically made for female roles, *laodan* roles, and eunuchs in the imperial palace.

Designated by the general term *tou kui* (头盔), Peking opera

Peking opera costumes

headdresses comprise such items as crowns, helmets, hats and scarves. Crowns are for the emperor and nobles; military officers and soldiers wear helmets, while ordinary folk sport soft scarves or straw hats. Some headgear, such as crowns, is rigid, while other is soft.

A wide variety of shoes and boots are used in Peking opera performances, mainly platform boots (*hou di xue,* 厚底靴), tiger-headed boots (*hu tou xue,* 虎头靴), thin-soled combat footwear made of black satin (*kuai xue,* 快靴), fish-head pugilist's shoes, laced boxer's shoes, etc.

As mentioned above, the performance of actors (and actresses) is

Peking opera costumes

the absolute core of Chinese opera, and all other elements, costumes, props and stage settings, are used to serve this purpose. Therefore, a principle to be followed on the traditional Chinese operatic stage is that of virtuality, meaning that real objects are avoided and virtual objects are used as props to reduce performance-related costs. Some objects need to be magnified (such as wine cups and seal boxes) while others are made to appear smaller (such as cities, sedan chairs and carriages); as previously mentioned, on the Chinese operatic stage artists represent the horse with a whip, and the boat with an oar.

In traditional Chinese opera, the props, called *qi mo* (砌末), function as an indication of the dramatic context. Sometimes, a very small *qi mo*, introduced on stage with a corresponding performance from the actors or a certain music, may be a potent indicator of context and atmosphere. A streamer can stand for a wine shop; a wooden knocker or a clock may be used to contrast with the quietness of a Buddhist temple, while an official seal or a wooden block to strike a table evoke the forbidding atmosphere of an official institution. In a word, there is a whole set of strict rules for the use of *qi mo* on the stage of traditional Chinese opera; the realness and virtuality, magnification or minimalism pertaining to the objects used as *qi mo* must follow these rules. The following are typical examples of *qi mo* on the Chinese operatic stage.

A table and two chairs are usually placed on stage as props of a decorative nature, indicating a room. For the audience, the space around the table and chairs may be a royal palace, a scholar's study, a court where suspects are tried, a military commander's tent, or even a noisy restaurant. These different settings can be told apart from the details in the decoration of the table and chairs. If it is a royal palace, there will be dragon patterns on the tablecloth, and if it is a study, the tablecloth will be of a light blue or light green color and embroidered with orchid blossoms. The table can serve as a bed, a support for observing a distant object from a great height, a bridge, a gate tower, a mountain, or even a cloud. The chair can serve as a weapon for the characters. In this way, the audience is given great room for imagination. The expression "A table and two chairs" has come to symbolize the principle of "less is more" in the performing art of Peking opera.

The stage curtain (*shou jiu*) is made of cloth or satin, and is embroidered with exquisite patterns. On an old-style operatic stage, the front of the stage extends forward, with three sides facing the audience. The other side is the backstage. The curtain hangs across the backstage, and on each side of the curtain is a curtained door for performers to enter or exit the stage. Coming onto the stage from the entrance door, an actor with full make-up and costume begins his performance, and at the conclusion of his performance, he goes off the stage through the exit door, which signals the end of a show or a transition into another part of a play. After modern theatre and Western-style stage settings were introduced into traditional Chinese *xiqu* in the year 1908, the old-style curtain became generally obsolete, and thus was called "*shou jiu*" (守旧 , literally "keeping the old"). Originally, the *shou jiu* was a cloth or satin curtain with beautiful embroideries, but in some theatres or stages set in wealthy households, there were wooden boards carved with design patterns functioning as entrance and exit doors, which were called "*ying*

Kao (warriors' suit of armor)

Kao (warriors' suit of armor)   Prop whips used in Peking opera

shou jiu" (hard curtain).

Bu cheng (布城, cloth city gate), *yun pian* (云片, cloud sheet) and *shan shi pian* (山石片, rock sheet). The *bu cheng* is a virtual city gate made of a cloth frame, around two meters high and three or four meters wide. In Peking opera, this cloth city gate is used to represent various city gates, city walls and city gate towers. In the play *The Empty City Ruse* (*kong cheng ji*,《空城计》), the character Zhuge Liang (based on a historical figure from the Three Kingdoms period) stands on a cloth city gate; seeing this prop, the audience immediately understands it to

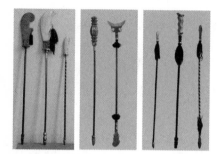

Peking opera stage props

symbolize a real city gate. The *yun pian* is a cloud-shaped sheet made of thick paper and white cloth, used in plays including legendary elements, in which characters fly through the sky. Similarly, the *shan shi pian* is a rock-shaped sheet made of cloth, usually fixed on a wooden frame. When the *shan shi pian* is part of a courtyard setting, it stands for the rockery which can often be found in a traditional Chinese courtyard; when put in front of the table, however, it symbolizes hills or rocky ridges.

Almost none of the stage props, big or small, including candlesticks, lanterns, oars, letters, paper, ink, writing brushes, ink slabs and pavilions, are real objects — they play a symbolic role only. A great variety of weapons, as well as the flags carried by honor guards, for instance, are also dummies. Within the perspective of virtuality, the unique artistic principle that differentiates traditional Chinese opera from Western drama, these stage props and settings are obviously essential in supporting that artistic principle.

Musical Accompaniment of Peking Opera

A Peking opera orchestra is divided into two parts: the *wen chang* (文场), whose main function is to accompany the singing, and the *wu chang* (武场), whose main function is to accompany the acting, speaking, dancing and acrobatic fighting. The music of the *wen chang* is dominated by a bowed string instrument called the *jing hu* (京胡, "Peking opera fiddle"), or *jing erhu* (京二胡, "two-string Peking opera fiddle"), and is supplemented by plucked string instruments such as the *yueqin* (月琴, "moon-shaped mandolin") and the *pipa* (琵琶, four-string Chinese lute). The *jing hu*, *jing erhu* and *yueqin* are called the *san da jian* (三大件, "three major instruments") of the Peking opera orchestra. The *jing hu* has a similar function as a musical instrument in Peking opera as the violin in the Western-style symphony, in the sense that the entire orchestra is led by the *jing hu* player. Every well-known singing actor of Peking opera usually has his personal *jing hu* player, who does not appear until the actor he serves comes onto the stage. The *jing hu* was introduced around the 50th year of Emperor Qianlong's reign (1785), when operatic artists adapted the *huqin* to suit the *pihuang* tunes of the then-burgeoning Peking opera. With its loud music tones, the sound of *jing hu* may best highlight the unique features of Peking opera and

Yue qin (moon-shaped mandolin) used in Peking opera   *Hu qin* (a stringed instrument)

the performers' singing style. The *jing erhu*, also called the *wengzi* (瓮子), is a stringed instrument of alto range, somewhat like the viola in the Western symphonic orchestra. Invented by Mei Lanfang and Wang Shaoqing, it is an adaption of the *erhu* made to suit the tunes of Peking opera; thanks to its full and mellow sound, it forms a beautiful contrast with the delicate tones of the *jing hu*. For a similar reason, this instrument is usually used to accompany the singing of *dan* roles. The *yueqin* is a musical instrument with a long history; it is said that it grew popular in the Jin Dynasty (265-420 AD), and that the name *yueqin* began to be used from the Tang Dynasty. A high-pitched instrument, the sound of the *yueqin* provides musical adornment to the melodies of the Peking opera orchestra.

In the *wu chang,* whose main function is to accompany the acting,

Performances of Peking opera

speaking, dancing and acrobatic fighting, percussion instruments predominate, including a variety of drums, wooden clappers, gongs and cymbals. The drummer heads the *wu chang* team of musicians and he also acts as the conductor of the entire orchestra, although he generally is not as well-known as the *jing hu* player, for it is the metric beats played by the drums and clappers that control the rhythm of the entire performance. The *wu chang* team produces music and creates different stage atmospheres.

A Peking opera performance is often accompanied by "a deafening sound of gongs and cymbals." People who are unfamiliar with traditional Chinese operas may find it very noisy. The origin of this loud music can be traced back to a time when theatrical companies used gongs and cymbals to attract audiences for performances set on top of makeshift stages, in the midst of the bustle of markets or streets. But in some Peking opera plays, Kunqu opera music, which is not as loud, can be used.

Singing is an important part of any Peking opera performance, and is closely connected with music. While the audience is focused on the performers on stage, and on their colorful costumes and acting, the *wen chang* and *wu chang* teams of musicians flanking the stage control the rhythm, the key to performance success. And of course, besides controlling the rhythm, the orchestra also provides the music itself. In traditional operatic theory, a good performance is said to "depend 30 percent on the front stage (acting and singing), and 70 percent on the back stage (music)." Besides, contrary to Western opera orchestras, which feature dozens of musicians and a special orchestra box on the stage, the Peking opera orchestra relies on no more than ten musicians to provide the melodious music which represents the most wonderful of all Chinese cultural traditions.

CHAPTER III
Sweet and Mellow Yueju Opera:
the Second Major Form of Traditional Chinese Opera

One of the five major forms of traditional Chinese opera, Yueju is regarded as only second to Peking opera in its influence. This form of opera is very popular in such areas as Zhejiang, Shanghai, Jiangsu and Fujian, and it is widely known and sung by people outside China. The theme at the heart of most Yueju plays is that of a romance taking place between a talented scholar and a beautiful girl. Although it encompasses many artistic singing and performing schools, this form of opera is generally renowned for its lyricism, and places particular emphasis on singing. Through delicate tunes and a moving performance, it exemplifies the sweet and mellow taste most favored by people south of the Yangtze River. On May 20, 2006, the incorporation of Yueju opera into the first list of Intangible Cultural Heritage was approved by the State Council of the People's Republic of China.

The History of Yueju Opera

Yueju opera originated in a tradition of Chinese folk singing[1] (*luo di changshu*, 落地唱书), an art form popular in Sheng County of Zhejiang Province, of which the earliest melodies were closely related to those of Buddhist "scroll proclaiming" (*xuan juan*, 宣卷). The art of *luo di changshu* was created in the second year of Emperor Xianfeng's reign (1852) by Jin Qibing, a peasant of Matang Village of West Township, Sheng County, and it later evolved into *ling a diao* (吟嗄调, literally "a tune featuring whispers and exclamations"), which kept on being sung until after Yueju opera took shape. From *luodi changshu* to Yueju opera, this operatic art form went through six distinct stages of evolution.

The Period of "*xiao ge ban*" (also called "*di du ban*")

On the Qingming Day of the thirtieth year of Emperor Guangxu's reign (1906), some folk actors from Dongwang Village of Sheng County, Zhejiang Province, including Gao Binghuo, Li Shiquan and Qian Jingsong, set up a temporary stage with door panels in front of the incense hall of the village, and performed the plays *Ten Prohibitions* (*shi jian tou*, 《十件头》) and *Double Golden Flowers* (*shuang jin hua*, 《双金花》);

---

[1] The Chinese term *changshu* 唱书 literally means "to sing (from) a book, to sing a story."

"Small tunes troupes" (*xiao ge ban*)

their costumes were simple, colorful robes and cotton skirts borrowed from their fellow villagers. This was the debut of local *changshu* artists in Sheng County, who formed troupes known as "small tunes and songs troupes" (*xiao ge wen shu ban*, 小歌文书班), or in short form, "small tunes troupes" (*xiao ge ban*, 小歌班), so as to differentiate them from operatic troupes of Shaoxing opera (*Shaoxing da ban*, 绍兴大班). Since then, more and more *changshu* artists performed on stage, and by the following year, there were many *xiao ge ban* troupes performing here and there all over the county. In the thirty-second year of Emperor Guangxu's reign (1908), *xiao ge ban* troupes spread outside the local area into three directions: to the northeast, they spread to Ningbo through Xinchang and Yuyao; to the southwest, they spread to Jinhua through Dongyang and Zhuji, and to the northwest, they spread to Hangzhou,

Yueju opera performers

Jiaxing and Huzhou area through Shangyu and Shaoxing. In the second year of Emperor Xuantong's reign (1910), the *xiao ge ban* troupes led by Qian Jingsong and others performed in Hangzhou.

The Period of Shaoxing Civil Opera as Performed by Troupes of Male Performers

Around 1916, *xiao ge ban* troupes gave a number of performances in Shanghai, and in 1920, over 40 artists representing these troupes came together and performed a series of new plays on the theme of women's oppression, which were welcomed by their Shanghai audience, including *The Tale of the Chinese Lute* (*pi pa ji*,《琵琶记》), *The Tragedy of Liang Shanbo and Zhu Yingtai* (*liang zhu ai shi*,《梁祝哀史》), *The Jade Hairpin*(*bi yu zan*,《碧玉簪》), and *Meng Lijun* (《孟丽君》). Thereafter, these *xiao ge ban* troupes gained a firm foothold in the city. In 1923, over 30 performers including Ma Chaoshui, Wang Yongchun, Ye Qinfang and Mei Yuelou left the Shengping Singing and Dancing Company and formed their own company. These performers later gave performances at the famous Great World Pleasure Ground in the name of "*Shaoxing Wenxi*" or "Shaoxing civil opera."

In this period of development, some important reforms were enacted within the operatic form in terms of music and performance. The artists assimilated the musical elements of Shaoxing opera, Yuyao tunes and

Poster for a Yueju opera show

Wulin tunes, and enriched the rhythmic structure of the opera. In particular, they created various tuning and rhythmic combinations such as *dao ban* (倒板, literally "reversed beats"), *kuai ban* (快板, literally "fast beats"), *qing ban* (清板, literally "clear beats") and *huan yang diao* (还阳调, literally "revived tunes"). After the good debut of the *xiao ge ban* troupes in Shanghai, the first professional *xiao ge ban* band was formed, which experimented with the use of string instruments to play the prelude and the interlude, and then to accompany the actors' singing. First they used the *banhu* (板胡), a bowed string instrument with a thin wooden soundboard, which was later replaced by another

Performance of the Yueju opera play *Liang Shanbo and Zhu Yingtai*

Typical Yueju opera moves

string instrument, the *pinghu* (平胡), for the music from the latter was milder and mellower. The string instrument was tuned to *do-sol*, which was called *zheng diao* (正调) or "standard tones," so that the period of Shaoxing civil opera as performed by male performers was also called the period of *"nan ban si xian zheng diao"* (男班丝弦正调), literally, "Shaoxing civil opera as performed by male performers with string instruments tuned to their standard tones." In terms of operatic tunes, the artists assimilated such styles as *"dao ban"* (导板, "guiding beats"), *"liu shui"* (流水, "flowing water") and *"si fan"* (思凡, "longing for the mortal world") from Shaoxing opera, and integrated them to *ling a diao*, so that separate tunes were given fixed beats. Eventually, a musical structure featuring a "beat-and-tune style" (*ban qiang ti*) took shape. In terms of performance, the artistic features of Shaoxing opera and Peking opera were also borrowed, and improvements made to the repertoire — playlets on everyday themes were abandoned, and more major costume plays were added. Shaoxing civil opera as performed by male performers thus entered its golden era.

The Period of Shaoxing Civil Opera as Performed by Troupes of Female Performers

In 1923, under the influence of *mao'er* opera (髦儿戏), a kind of Peking opera performed solely by female performers, which was popular in Shanghai, the owner of the Shengping Singing and Dancing Company, Wang Jinshui, entrusted performer Jin Rongshui to form the first professional female performing troupe. After a short period of training, the troupe began to give performances in Shanghai under the names "Shaoxing Civil Operatic Troupe" (绍兴文戏) and "Female Troupe Performing Both Civil and Military Plays" (文武女班); female troupes performing civil plays then mushroomed after the year 1928. Due to the fact that the vocal range of female singers was four or five notes higher than that of male singers, the string player Wang Chunrong examined

the vocal characteristics of female performers,
assimilated the *xipi* style of Peking opera, and tuned
his instrument to *la-mi*, hence the "*si* and *gong*
tones" (四工调), thus called because the notes *la*
and *mi* are called "*si*" and "*gong*," respectively, in
traditional Chinese musical notation. Consequently,
the period of Shaoxing civil opera as performed by
female performers is also called the period of *si*
and *gong* tones. In the first female troupe, female
performers sometimes went on stage together with
male performers in their traveling performances, a

A Yueju opera perfor-
mance

practice known in the history of Yueju opera as that of "performances by
both male and female performers" (in Shanghai, some female performers,
the most famous being Bai Yumei Junior, had been on stage together
with male performers). By learning the performing techniques from male
performers and assimilating the artistic strength of Shaoxing operatic
troupes, the first female performers of Yueju opera made great progress
in terms of singing style and performance. The most famous among
them was Shi Yinhua (1910-1984), a pioneer of female-acting Yueju opera,
who was later regarded as the "*hua shan bi zu*" (花衫鼻祖), or "female
ancestor" of Yueju opera. In 1929, the second troupe consisting solely
of female performers, the Jinxin Performing Company (锦新舞台), was

Photo of a show of Yueju opera

情探

剧情介绍

秀才王魁，因投亲不遇，流落异乡，病倒在雪地上。名
妓桂英将其救起并资助他读书。二人结为夫妇。后王魁赴京
赶考得中状元。黄黄弄桂英入赘相府，而谁给桂英一纸休书。
桂英控诉无门，含冤自杀。她的灵魂至京都寻找王魁，以请
求收留之情进行试探，不料王魁竟要加害于她。桂英忍无可
忍，活捉了王魁。

Poster for a Yueju opera show

formed in Huangze of Sheng County, and from 1930, many female troupes were formed in Sheng County, among which the Qunying Performing Company (群英舞台). Since 1933, these female companies became increasingly popular in Shanghai, and performed in teahouses and hotels. And starting from 1936, female troupes finally replaced male troupes and became widely accepted in Zhejiang Province and Shanghai, due to the fact that female performers were beautiful in appearance and their voices sweet and flowing. The term "Shaoxing civil opera as performed by female performers" was replaced by that of "Yueju opera" in the autumn of 1938. According to statistics, in September 1939 there were 13 female troupes

Yueju opera performance

of Shaoxing civil opera active in Shanghai, and at the beginning of 1941, there were 34 female Yueju opera troupes in Shanghai, outnumbering by far other local opera troupes. On the eve of the Anti-Japanese War (1937-1945), Shanghai was the heart of Yueju opera, and almost all well-known performers were performing in this metropolis. The artistic skills of female Yueju opera performers improved ever further, and a number of great and influential performers emerged. In 1942, Yuan Xuefen (1922-2011), a leading performer and the founder of the Yuan School of Yueju opera, initiated in-depth reforms of the Yueju opera tradition at the Dalai Theatre, engaging Lü Zhong, Han Yi and Zheng Chuanjian as directors, replacing the scene plot system by a play script, laying the foundation of a director-centered system, conducting reforms regarding costumes and make-up, and improving stage settings and light. She rendered band structure more comprehensive, and together with the musicians, created the *chi diao qiang* (尺调腔) — *sol* being known as *he chi* (合尺) in traditional Chinese musical notation — where the strings are tuned to *sol-re* with the basic tone of the tunes set at G, and which became the new basic tones of Yueju opera. In terms of performance, the performers assimilated the artistic skills of Kunqu opera and Western drama, and thus largely enriched and developed Yueju opera.

The Period of Artistic Reform of Yueju Opera

As mentioned above, Yuan Xuefen initiated a reform of Yueju opera in October 1942 under the banner of "new Yueju opera," and in March 1945, the Xuesheng Troupe (雪声剧团), a new operatic troupe led by Yuan Xuefen and Fan Ruijuan, was formed. Reforms were conducted in other performing troupes as well. These reforms greatly changed the operatic system of Yueju opera in terms of performing styles and stage mechanisms. It is worth a special mention that a number of new-style writers and artists helped promote the reform of Yueju opera. After Yuan Xuefen started advocating operatic reform in the autumn of 1942, each troupe promoting the "new Yueju opera" established a department of stage affairs, recruiting new-style writers and artists to work as playwrights, directors, composers and stage artistic designers. The first intellectuals to participate in the operatic reform drew artistic essence

Yueju opera body postures

Yueju opera body postures

from new-style literature, Western drama and film, and introduced new artistic concepts and expression techniques into Yueju opera. The scene plot system was replaced by the play script system, and all the performed plays were newly written or adapted traditional ones. In terms of stage art, the traditional system — involving explanations about how a part or scene should be acted — was abandoned, in favor of a director-centered system. The new performance style, which borrowed techniques from drama and film, laid more emphasis on the depiction of the personality and psychology of the characters, while simultaneously integrating body movements from Kunqu and other operas. In the musical aspect, the position of composer was established within the operatic troupe, and for each new play, a singing style and musical accompaniment would be created, according to the specific content of the play and designed to suit specific characters. In terms of stage art, the stage wardrobe and *shou jiu* (old-style stage curtain) were abandoned, and the costumes started to be designed according to the specific plot and characters. Paints began to be used for make-up, and stage light and stage effect equipment as well as comprehensive stage settings were adopted.

In May 1946, the Xuesheng Troupe performed the play *Xianglin's Wife* (*xiang lin sao*《祥林嫂》), adapted from Lu Xun's well-known novel, *New Year Sacrifice* (*zhu fu*《祝福》), which was a milestone and a remarkable achievement in the reform of Yueju opera. After Shanghai

Performance of the Yueju opera play *Xianglin's Wife*

was liberated, some Yueju operatic troupes advocating reform, originating from Shanghai and Simingshan, merged and formed the East China Yueju Experimental Troupe in April 1950, which was placed under the direct leadership of the East China Department of Culture. In March 1951, the East China Institute of Operatic Research was established, and the year 1954 saw the foundation of the Zhejiang Yueju Opera Troupe. During this period of time, more than 30 professional Yueju opera troupes from Shanghai and over 70 professional troupes from Zhejiang experienced reform in all aspects of the operatic system.

In the 1950s, a number of high-level plays were created, in which the direction, performance, music and stage art were all greatly improved. On the first National Traditional Opera Festival, held in 1952, *Liang*

Yueju opera performance

Shanbo and Zhu Yingtai (《梁山伯与祝英台》), *A Tale of the White Snake* (*bai she zhuan*,《白蛇传》) and *A Tale of the West Chamber* (*xi xiang ji*,《西厢记》) were praised for their excellence. In 1955, the Shanghai Yueju Troupe was established; it readapted and performed *Xianglin's Wife* the next year to express the original message from Lu Xun's novel. In 1962 the play was further adapted and modified, thus becoming a perfect Yueju opera play in both its ideological content and artistic style.

Artistic Characteristics of Yueju Opera

Yueju Opera Tunes and Music

Yueju opera adopts a musical structure of "beat-and-tune style" (*ban qiang ti*). While the art form still belonged to the "folk singing" (*luodi changshu*) stage of its development, the music featured rather monotonous melodies, similar to indigenous folk songs. When *luodi chan shu* evolved into *ling a diao* after assimilating the tunes of *san tiao* (三跳 "three beats," thus called because its accompanying music involves three beats of clapper) originating in Huzhou, it was divided into "north *ling a diao*" (吟嗄北调) and "south *ling a diao*" (吟嗄南调). The "north *ling a diao*" was mild and sweet, and "south *ling a diao*" was open and straightforward. Apart from *san tiao*, other tunes of local art forms were also integrated into *ling a diao*, including the "*duan gong* tune" of *tan huang* (滩簧, a folk art form) originating in Yuyao, as well as the "*qian tang* tune," "*shizi* tune" and "*aiai* tune" of folk songs from Hangzhou and the surrounding area. When standard tones of *ban hu* were adopted to accompany *ling a diao* in 1920, Yueju opera entered the period of *si xian zheng diao*, meaning performers were accompanied with string instruments tuned to their standard tones.

The singing, in the various schools of Yueju opera, consists of two parts: melodies and singing style. As for the melodic structure, each school has its own distinct methods, in which various melodies, rhythms and beats are combined to form different basic styles. Keys to the artistic characteristics of each school are the rising and falling tunes, the delay between different lines and at the end of each line, as well as the characteristic musical language and habitual tones that are constantly repeated and changing. As for the singing style, each school of Yueju opera tries to show its originality in terms of articulation, tones and expressiveness, so that different artistic flavors can be created through the performers' articulation, including distinctive tones and melodic ornaments. Some nuances in their tunes include many special singing formats that cannot be recorded with available notations, but these may even better exemplify the distinctive flavors of each school's singing styles.

Stylized Performance of Yueju Opera

In early development stages, after the *xiao ge ban* troupes appeared, the performance of Yueju opera was quite simple. The different *changshu* tones had been abandoned and replaced by the performance of different roles in the play. The major form of performance was singing, and there were few gestures or body movements, as a remaining characteristic of *changshu* performances. Later, the performers of this operatic form enriched their performing skills in two aspects: when performing playlets on everyday themes, they would imitate everyday movements with a little artistic refinement, such as picking tealeaves, threading and sewing, cooking, appreciating flowers or beautiful scenes, and riding animals. And when performing major costumed plays, the basic stylized body movements of other operas (mainly those of Shaoxing opera) were borrowed, for instance when opening a door, closing a window, climbing stairs, boating, sitting in a sedan chair, riding a horse, etc. In this period, strict performing conventions for Yueju opera had not yet taken shape.

In the period of Shaoxing civil plays (by male and later female performers), at the beginning of the 1940s, when Yueju opera began to be performed in major cities, the performers learned from Peking opera and Shaoxing opera and gradually conventionalized performance body movements. Some troupes even invited performers of military plays of Peking opera to teach performers martial arts. After female troupes became popular, many troupes established a system to learn the performing skills of civil plays from Shaoxing opera, and learn those of military plays from Peking opera. Apprentices had to learn various stylized movements requiring high-level skills, and it was during this period that some performers realized they should try to give expression to the personalities and psychologies of different characters.

The reform of Yueju opera initiated by Yuan Xuefen in the autumn

Yueju opera performance

Yueju opera performance

of 1942 brought some major innovations to the operatic form. On the one hand, it assimilated the essence of Western drama and film art and sought to depict the personalities and psychologies of characters, paying more attention to the true-to-life expression of emotions. On the other hand, it learned beautiful dancing movements and stylized body movements from Kunqu opera and Peking opera, so that the gestures and body movements of performers became more refined and rhythmic. The combination of these two aspects thus formed the special performing style of Yueju opera, featuring a seamless integration of dramatic realism and expressionism.

After the founding of the People's Republic of China in 1949, the development of Yueju opera put more emphasis on the combination of dramatic realism and expressionism, meaning the expression of characters' state of mind through the beautified body movements of performers. Attaching strong importance to overall stage effect, the artistic pursuit of Yueju opera lies in characterization through true-to-life performance and rich and precise body movements. Some of the best examples include the characters Cui Yingying and Xianglin's wife impersonated by Yuan Xuefen; Qu Yuan and Liang Yushu impersonated by Yin Guifang; Liang Shanbo and Zheng Yuanhe impersonated by Fan Ruijuan; Fu Guiying impersonated by Fu Quanxiang; Jia Baoyu impersonated by Xu Yulan and Lin Daiyu impersonated by Wang Wenjuan. In the case of modern figures, the Yueju opera performance emphasizes the representation of a character's individuality by integrating real-to-life depiction and larger-than-life performance. Yueju performers in Zhejiang have refined many everyday movements into stylized performance movements, and their artistic exploration in this aspect has not yet come to an end.

CHAPTER IV
Natural and Simple Yu Opera:
The Local Opera with the Largest Number of Performers

Henan opera, known as "Yu opera," is the local opera with the largest number of performers. Since the turn of the millennium, this local opera has counted the largest number of professional and amateur troupes, and in its heyday, there were over 300 professional Yu opera troupes in almost every province, autonomous region and municipality, including Tibet, in addition to numerous amateur troupes. Yu opera was called "*Henan bangzi*" (河南梆子, "Henan clapper") or "*Henan gao diao*" (河南高调, "Henan high-pitched tunes") in the past. And since in earlier times, performers sung most tunes in chest voice and used falsetto to sing the end syllable at the beginning and the end of tunes and made it sound like a short "o," the opera was also called "Henan O" (河南讴). The name "Yu opera" was originally used to refer to all operatic forms sung in Henan, until the autumn of 1947, when the mass media of Luoyang, Kaifeng, Lanzhou and Xi'an began to use this name when referring to Henan *bangzi*.

This form of opera was officially given the name "Yu opera" in 1952, as a result of the efforts of several generations of operatic artists before and

after the founding of the People's Republic of China, who reformed and brought innovations to Henan *bangzi*. This was a significant event in the history of Henan opera, and it marked the beginning of its development and prospering as a systematic operatic art.

Yu opera is popular in more than a dozen provinces and regions in China, including Henan, Hebei, Shandong, Shanxi, Hubei, Shaanxi, Gansu, Xinjiang, Taiwan, Anhui, Qinghai, Sichuan and Jiangsu, and it is one of the most influential local operas in China.

On May 20, 2006, the incorporation of Yu opera into the first list of Intangible Cultural Heritage was approved by the State Council of the People's Republic of China.

The History of Yu Opera

Originally, there were three main versions of the origin of Yu opera. One held that after the Qinqiang and Puzhou *bangzi* spread into the Henan area during the late Ming Dynasty, they were integrated with local folk songs and tunes and evolved into Yu opera. The second version stated that it had developed from *xian suo diao* (弦索调) of the system of northern tunes. And the third version insisted that Yu opera originated in the art of Henan *changshu*, and that after the mid and late Ming Dynasty, in particular, it had been developed from the short songs popular in the Central Plains area by assimilating the artistic achievements of the *xian suo diao*, among other tunes.

A character from the Yu opera play *Picking Firewood* (*jian chai*)

However, extensive research and in-depth analysis carried out over a great amount of historical material, especially in the compilation process of the *Annals of Chinese Local Operas – Henan*, led experts

A character in the play *Mulian Saving His Mother* (*mu lian jiu mu*)

to conclude that Henan *bangzi* originated in Kaifeng and surrounding counties. That Yu opera originated in Kaifeng is by no means coincident. Kaifeng is indeed a famous historical city, known for its rich cultural heritage and its diversity in the field of entertainment arts. In the Song Dynasty (960-1279), especially, when Kaifeng was capital of the country, theatres, entertainment facilities and markets were found everywhere. In *Reminiscences of the Eastern Capital* (*dong jing meng hua lu*, 《东京梦华录》), a local historical record of Kaifeng city, there are many references to various pleasure houses and theatres that could accommodate an audience of several thousand. By that time, a large-scale *zaju*, *Mulian Saving His Mother* (*Mulian jiu mu*,《目连救母》

), had already been performed in Kaifeng. Obviously, modern Yu opera experienced a development of about a thousand years, from *gan bangzi* (干梆子, literally "clapper rap without musical accompaniment") to *tu bangzi* (土梆子, literally "local clapper tunes"), finally turning into Henan *bangzi*.

According to certain Henan opera performers, when they began to learn their art, around 1912, they heard that "Henan O" was already popular in the "Inner Ten Counties" and the "Outer Eight Counties" during the Ming and Qing dynasties. It is said that the earliest teachers of Henan opera were either from the Jiang or from the Xu families, the Jiangs being located in Zhuxian Town, to the south of Kaifeng, and

Yu opera performance

Performance of the Yu opera play *Hong Niang the Maidservant* (*hong niang*)

A character from the Yu opera play *Cosmos Point* (*Yu Zhou Feng*)

the Xus in Qingheji, to the east of Kaifeng. Both families recruited apprentices and organized operatic troupes. Legend has it that the so-called "three earliest Henan opera troupes" of Kaifeng, namely the Yicheng Troupe, the Gongyi Troupe and the Gongxing Troupe, were all established before the Ming Dynasty.

According to *Lamp in the Side-Street* (*qi lu deng*,《岐路灯》), completed by Li Lüyuan in the forty-second year of Emperor Qianlong's reign (1777) and *The Annals of Qi County* (《杞县志》), published in the fifty-third year of Emperor Qianlong's reign (1788), at that time *bangzi* opera was already popular around Kaifeng and Qi County, and the performers often joined those of *luo xi* (罗戏) and *juan xi* (卷戏) (both local operatic forms), which led the performances to be known as *"bang luo juan."* As is recorded in the inscriptions on local tablets, it was in the imperial palace of the Ming Dynasty that "various operatic troupes performed, prayed and attended banquets, and due to their great age it is not known when exactly they first came into being. During the reign of Emperor Daoguang (1821-1850) the river dyke breached and swept away all the temples." From this we can see that *bangzi* opera was already sung before Emperor Daoguang's reign.

After the Xinhai Revolution that overthrew the Qing Dynasty, performers of Henan *bangzi* gave more performances in cities. At that time the famous teahouses, such as Zhixiang Teahouse, Puqing Teahouse, Chenghuai Teahouse, Qing Teahouse, Donghuo Temple Teahouse, or Tongle Teahouse, vied with each other to invite or employ performing troupes to give performances of Henan *bangzi*, so that the troupes became quite popular at the time, among which the Yicheng Troupe, the Tianxing Troupe, the Gongyi Troupe and the Gongxing Troupe. Later, more teahouses where Henan *bangzi* opera was performed appeared in cities like Zhengzhou, Luoyang, Xinyang and Shangqiu. In the countryside, whenever there were sacrifice ceremonies or festivals, Henan operatic plays were performed, and in some areas, most of the plays performed were Henan *bangzi*. In the late 1920s and early 1930s, Henan

Yu opera performance

bangzi entered a new chapter of development. During this period, four theatres were successively established in Xiangguo Temple of Kaifeng, namely Yong'an Theatre, Yongle Theatre, Yongmin Theatre and Tongle Theatre, and many well-known performers of Henan *bangzi*, including Chen Suzhen, Wang Runzhi, Ma Shuangzhi, Si Fengying, Li Ruiyun, Chang Xiangyu, Zhao Yiting and Peng Haibao, gathered in Kaifeng to perform.

In the beginning of 1935, Fan Cuiting led other artists to establish the Yusheng Theatrical Society (豫声戏剧学社) and changed the name of Yongle Theatre into Yusheng Theatre. Both the Qi County Troupe of Henan and the Cao County Troupe of Shandong, where Chen Suzhen and Zhao Yiting belonged, respectively, joined the Yusheng Theatrical Society. This theatrical society reformed Henan *bangzi* by abandoning some outdated practices of old-style performing troupes, and adding innovations to the performance and stage arts; it also performed new plays created by Fan Cuiting, including *The Soaring Aspirations (ling yun zhi,*《凌云志》), *Righteousness Matters (yi lie feng,*《义烈风》), *The Greatest Injustice (xiao rang hen,*《霄壤恨》), *Revenge by Death (di chi xue,*《涤耻血》) and *Departing Three Times (sa fu xiu,*《三拂袖》). In 1938, after the outbreak of the Anti-Japanese War, the theatrical society changed its name to "Shihou Opera Troupe" (狮吼剧团), with "Shihou" literally meaning "the howl of a lion," conveying the idea that the Chinese people, invaded by Japanese invaders, were full of rage like an awakened lion.

In 1936, Chang Xiangyu (1922-2004) went to Kaifeng as a performer of Zhou Haishui's performing troupe, and began to perform at Xingyu Theatre. In 1937, Chang Xiangyu quit Zhou's troupe and began to perform within the newly established Zhongzhou Operatic Research Society (中州戏曲研究社), a performing troupe initiated by Chang's father and several others, including Wang Zhennan, who wrote costumed plays such as *The Tale of the West Chamber — Six Selected Scenes (liu bu xi xiang,*《六部西厢》) and *Weeping at the Great Wall(ku chang cheng,* 《哭长城》),   as well as *Beating the Land (da tu di,*《打土地》), a modern play on the theme of the Japanese invasion. *Beating the Land* was the first modern play of Yu opera. Meanwhile, performers like Wang Runzhi, Ma Shuangzhi, Peng Haibao and Yang Jinyu also performed a number of traditional plays at Yong'an Theatre. This gathering of well-known performers accelerated the integration of eastern Henan tunes (*yu dong diao,* 豫东调) and western Henan tunes (*yu xi diao,* 豫西调), and promoted the development of Henan *bangzi* as a mature operatic art.

After the Japanese army occupied Kaifeng in 1938, the Shihou Opera Troupe, the Taiyi Troupe led by Zhou Haishui, along with other troupes and performers, including Chang Xiangyu, went to Xi'an and to perform there and in other northwestern provinces and regions, thus greatly

Yu opera performance

expanding the influence of Henan *bangzi*. From that time until the founding of the People's Republic of China in 1949, many Henan *bangzi* troupes were found in Xi'an, including the Shihou Opera Troupe, led by Fan Cuiting, the Xiangyu Troupe (香玉剧社) led by Chang Xiangyu, the Fenglin Troupe (凤麟剧团) led by Mao Lanhua, the Languang Troupe (兰光剧社) led by Cui Lantian, as well as the Disaster-hit Children's Operatic Society (河南灾童戏剧学社), predecessor of the former Tibetan Henan Opera Troupe.

After the founding of the People's Republic of China, many professional Yu opera performing troupes were established all over Chinese mainland, and many new melodies and plays were created. The central government has also helped produce a large number of documentary films and telefilms to document and record the performances of many artists and troupes. The Henan Yu Opera Troupe was established in March 1956, and on September 8 of the same year, the Henan Provincial Bureau of Culture proposed to search and collect traditional plays and decided to hold the First Henan Provincial Traditional Opera Festival at the end of that year. During the festival held in December that year, 23 traditional opera forms were represented altogether, almost half of which as Yu opera plays. In the mid-1950s, many professional Yu opera performing troupes were established all over China, and it became one of the most influential forms of local opera in China.

Artistic Characteristics of Yu Opera

Yu Opera Tunes and Music

Yu opera is an operatic form that puts more emphasis on singing than on any other element. The singing style of Yu opera is forceful and full of energy, making it well suited to the expression of passionate and deeply felt emotions. Thanks to its simple and natural qualities, Yu opera is easily enjoyed by ordinary people, and thus it may accommodate both small comedies and full-scale costumed and historical plays. Performers usually use big-clapper tunes (*da ban* tunes) for the key plots of Yu opera plays, which feature a flowing singing style, crisp beats and clear articulation of lyrics, so that they can be easily understood by the audience.

The musical structure of Yu opera can be classified as *ban shi bian hua ti*, or "changing metric-type style" (板式变化体), and includes four major metric types, namely the double eight-beat (*er ba ban*, one strong beat and one weak beat), the slow beat (*man ban*, one strong beat and three weak beats), the fastest beat (*liu shui ban*, "flowing-water beat") and the unfixed beat (*san ban*).

Among the four metric types listed above, the double eight-beat is the most expressive and has the most variants. It is so-called because in the old days, Yu opera was based on repetitions of a period of two eight-beat tunes (eight bars). Following the development of Yu opera,

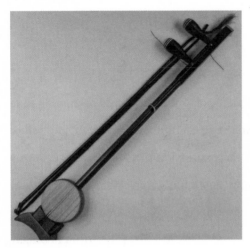

Banhu (fiddle)   *Tang gu* (war drum)

artists modified this fixed metric type. Today's double eight-beat metric style shows the integration between eastern Henan tunes and Western Henan tunes; when based on "one strong beat and one weak beat" (*yi ban yi yan*, 一板一眼, which corresponds to the quick and simple 2/4 of Western music), a lengthy aria can include over a hundred lines, which explains why this metric type is often used in narrative songs. And since there are many variants to the basic "one strong beat and one weak beat" with varying speed, it can be used to express a broad range of emotions according to the dramatic plot.

The slow beat also has a number of variants, but it usually consists of one strong beat and three weak beats, corresponding to the quick, simple

<table>
2
1 3 4
</table>

1. *Ban gu* (a small drum for marking time)
2. Bass gongs
3. *Er ba ban* clappers
4. Yu opera band

4/4 time of Western music. As one of the four commonly seen metric types of Yu opera, there are multiple types of prelude and interlude for this metric style. Its basic structure is as follows: each phrase is usually divided into two lines, with an interlude in between; and after the whole phrase is sung, an ending interlude is placed at the end of it. However, there may be some variants to this basic structure, and the speed can also vary, like that of the double eight-beat, to express different feelings according to the plot.

The fastest beat (*liu shui ban*), as its name implies, also has several variants that differ as to speed. Songs following this metric type also feature one strong beat immediately after one weak beat, and it can be used quite flexibly for different melodies, to express either cheerful and light-hearted emotions or grievous and depressed states of mind. The metric type's most obvious characteristic is that it frequently features syncopated rhythm that crosses music bars, so that the beginning and ending of each line, as well as the transitions in the melodies, may correspond with the weak beat. There are many varying beginning and ending forms for tunes of this metric type.

The unfixed beat (*san ban*, 散板) is also called "non-beat" (*fei ban*, 非板), for there is no fixed strong or weak beat for this metric type. Accents do not occur at regular intervals of a bar but rather, their positions often depend on the pitch and the duration of the note. Usually songs using this metric type are very short, with only four, six or eight lines.

For all the above four metric types, the lyrics are either ten-character rhymed verses arranged in a 3/3/4 form or seven-character rhymed verses arranged in a 2/2/3 form. Sometimes verses with other arrangements or without any fixed character arrangement are also used. For example, in *gua da zui* (呱嗒嘴), a variant of the double eight-beat metric type, a five-character verse is used, and in *gun bai* (滚白), a variant of the unfixed beat, lines in prose may combine songs and recitation.

Band and Musical Accompaniment of Yu Opera

In the earlier period of development of the art form, the main instruments used for civil plays of Yu opera were the *daxian* (大弦

, or *yueqin*, a lute with an octagonal sound box; the player of this instrument doubles as the *suona* player in the band), the *erxian* (二弦, a high-pitched bowed string instrument with a thin bamboo or wooden soundboard and paulownia wood surface), and the *sanxian* (三弦, a plucked string instrument). In the 1930s, Mr. Fan Cuiting borrowed from Shandong *bangzi* opera, introducing the *banhu* (a bowed string instrument) into Yu opera, and gradually abandoning the *erxian* to establish the mid-ranged *ban hu* as the principal musical instrument. After the 1950s, the *erhu*, *pipa*, bamboo flute, *sheng*, *menzi* (闷子) and cello were introduced into Yu opera civil plays, and later a number of Western instruments, including the electronic organ, violin, viola, as well as Western brass and woodwind instruments also appeared within Yu opera bands, so that they now feature an integration of traditional Chinese and Western instruments.

There are over 300 fixed accompanying melodies for civil plays of Yu opera, of which over 130 are played with the *suona* (a Chinese trumpet), over 20 are played with the horizontal flute and over 170 are played with string instruments.

The major instruments used for military plays of Yu opera include the *bangu* (板鼓, a small drum for marking time), the *tanggu* (堂鼓, war drum), the bass gong, the hand cymbal, the gong, and the wooden clapper. There are three major types of gong and drum rhythms in the military

plays of Yu opera. The first is that for the beginning of the performance. The second is used to accompany the body movements of performers or to build up atmosphere to suit a dramatic scene, most of which are the same as those used in Peking opera, but under different names. And the third is used to accompany singing, with special characteristics of Yu opera. Since there are many kinds of tunes for the four major metric types in Yu opera, these military plays benefit from no less than 100 gong and drum rhythms.

Role Categories and Performance of Yu Opera

There are four role categories in Yu opera: *sheng* (male roles), *dan* (female roles), *jing* (roles with painted face) and *chou* (clowns), and usually there are four *sheng* roles, four *dan* roles and four *jing* (*hua lian*) roles, so that in a traditional Yu opera troupe, there are "four types of *sheng*, four types of *dan* and four types of *jing* to play four soldiers, four generals and four servant girls; then there are eight instrument players (one drum player, two gong players, three *xian zi* players, one clapper player and one hand cymbal player) and two clowns." The four *sheng* roles include the *lao sheng* (old male roles), the *da hong lian* (or red *sheng*, literally "big red face," referring to the character Guan Yu), the *er hong lian* (literally "second red face," referring to other heroic characters in military plays) and the *xiao sheng*. The four types of *dan*

Yu opera performance

roles include the *zheng dan* (starring female roles, also called *qing yi*), the *xiao dan* (younger female roles, also called *hua dan* and *gui men dan*), the *lao dan* (old female roles) and the *shuai dan* (roles of female generals). The four types of *hua lian* include the *hei tou* (literally "black head," or *fu jing*), the first-rank *hua lian,* the second-rank *hua lian* and the third-rank *hua lian* (clown). And there are also troupes including five types of *sheng* roles, five types of *dan* roles and five types of *hua lian* roles. Most performers have a special line of business, while some performers may specialize in one role category but also play other types of roles.

Performers in each line of business have their own strict rules to follow. For instance, concerning hand gestures, "*hua lian* roles must raise their hands over their heads, *hong lian* to their eyebrows, *xiao sheng* to their lips and *xiao dan* to their chests." In military plays, close fighting should be performed through "quick body and eye movements, as well as brisk punches and swift kicks; all movements must be steady, abrupt, brave, swift and fast." There is also a number of different sets of movements in playing with weapons. For *gui men dan* (unmarried female roles), the rules are "when entering the stage, to extend your hands as if chasing geese, then to withdraw your hands while letting your water sleeves fall onto your wrists; to bow supply as if picking a small baby up, and when kneeling down, your ankles should not be seen by the audience;" "to talk without making eye contact, to walk without kicking your skirts; male and female shall not join hands, and you must sit down with your eyes on the side opening of your dress." For *cai dan* (female clown) roles, the rules are "to squint and peep at people, biting your lips when talking; with each twist your whole body shall move, and you must toss your handkerchief when walking." Each time a *xiao dan* (younger female role) enters the stage, the rules are "to press your temple with one hand, arranging your collar with both hands; to collect your embroidered shoes when bowing down, and then making neat the border of your dress." For *xiao sheng* roles, the rules are "to be handsome, neat and pushful," meaning the performers must have a handsome appearance, clear articulation, refined manners, neat and precise movements and an elevated spirit.

CHAPTER V
Loud and Vehement Qinqiang:
The Local Opera with the Longest History in China

Qinqiang (literally "Qin tunes"), or Shaanxi opera, is the oldest of all Chinese operas that are still in existence today. It is said that it was called "Emperor Qin Shihuang's Opera" during the Tang period, and later renamed Qinqiang. It boasts the largest, most ancient and diverse musical system of all Chinese operas. Qinqiang originated in Xifu (literally "western capital") during the Western Zhou Dynasty (the core area being today's Fengxiang and Qishan within Baoji Prefecture, therefore called "Western Qinqiang"). Also known as *luan tan* (literally "random/ disorderly play"), Qinqiang is popular in Shaanxi, Gansu, Qinghai, Ningxia and Xinjiang in northwest China. The *Xifu* Qinqiang tunes of Baoji are considered the oldest, for they still include many ancient words. Since jujube-wood clappers (*bangzi*) are used as instruments to beat time, the opera is also called "*bangzi* tunes," or popularly known as *guang guang zi* ("guang" being the word to imitate the sound of clappers). On May 20, 2006, the incorporation of Shaanxi opera into the first list of Intangible Cultural Heritage was approved by the State Council of the People's Republic of China.

The History of Qinqiang Opera

Qinqiang originated from ancient folk songs and dances around the area along the Yellow River Valley, nowadays corresponding to Shaanxi and Gansu provinces, and it experienced great development in Chang'an (today's Xi'an), one of the main political, economic and cultural centers of ancient China. The Central Shaanxi Plain has been referred to under the abbreviation "Qin" (秦) ever since the Zhou Dynasty (1100-221 B.C.), which is why this opera is called "Qinqiang," meaning "Qin tunes." In his *Yucun's Remarks on Operas* (*yu cun ju hua,*《雨村剧话》), Li Tiaoyuan (1734-1803), an opera theorist of the Qing Dynasty whose courtesy name was Yucun, wrote: "The popular story goes that the term Qinqiang appeared in Qian's *Zhuibaiqiu Collection of Operas*(*zhui bai qiu wai ji,*《缀百裘外集》), and originated in Shaanxi. In this opera, clappers are used to beat time and *yueqin* (a lute with an oval or octagonal sound box) as a musical instrument to accompany the tunes. Sometimes the rhythm is fast and sometimes it is slow. It is popularly called '*bangzi* opera', and is called *luan tan* by people in Sichuan." The term "*luan tan*" was widely used to refer to traditional operatic tunes in China; for a time it was used to refer to all forms of opera except Kunqu and high-pitched tunes (*gaoqiang*), and some used it to refer to Peking opera. Some local operas are given the name "*luan tan*," such as

A character of Qinqiang opera

Wenzhou *luan tan* and Hebei *luan tan*, but this term is most commonly used to refer to *bangzi* tunes, and thus to Qinqiang.

Qinqiang "originated in the Qin Dynasty, made great progress in the Han Dynasty, prospered in the Tang Dynasty, matured in the Yuan Dynasty, culminated in the Ming Dynasty and widely spread in the Qing Dynasty. Throughout its thousand-year history, it developed into a remarkable operatic form." This ancient form of opera is regarded as the oldest of traditional Chinese *xiqu*. In *The Lotus in the Monk's Alms Bowl* (*bo zhong lian*,《钵中莲》), a romance transcript dated to

Qinqiang opera performances

the Wanli period of the Ming Dynasty (1573-1620), there is an aria giving clear indication that it should be sung to the tune "*Er Fan* of Western Qinqiang" ([西秦腔二犯]); its lyrics consist of seven-character couplets, an evidence that Qinqiang had already spread to other areas at that time.

It is due to the fact that it spread all over the northwestern region of China that Qinqiang later evolved into different schools: Eastern Qinqiang (also called "Tongzhou *bangzi*," "old Qinqiang" or "Eastern

Characters of Qinqiang opera

bangzi"), popular in Dali and Pucheng of the Weinan area in the eastern part of the Central Shaanxi Plain; Western Qinqiang (also called "*Xifu* Qinqiang" or "western *bangzi*") popular in Fengxiang, Qishan and Longxian under Baoji Prefecture, in the Western part of the Central Shaanxi Plain and Tianshui of Gansu Province; *Handiao guangguang* (汉调桄桄 "*Guangguang* with Han tunes," also known as Southern Qinqiang, "Qinqiang with Han tunes" or *Guangguang* opera), popular in

Yang County, Chenggu, the Hantai area and Mian County of Hanzhong, in the south of Shaanxi Province; Northern Qinqiang (also called " ē *gong qiang*", 阿宫腔 or "è*gong qiang*", 遏宫腔) and popular in Qian County, Liquan, Fuping, Jingyang, Sanyuan and Lintong; and Central Qinqiang (Xi'an *luan tan*), popular in Xi'an. After Western Qinqiang spread to Sichuan, it coexisted with *deng xi* (灯戏, "lantern opera") and high-pitched tunes popular in Sichuan for a long time, before they were integrated into a unique *Sichuan bangzi* opera sung in Sichuan dialect, which is called *tanxi* (弹戏). Eastern Qinqiang also played a role in the development of such operatic forms as Peking opera, Shanxi opera, Yu opera, and Hebei *bangzi*. Due to the influence of local dialects and folk music of different areas, these schools of Qinqiang all differ as regards the pronunciations, tunes and music each of them advocates. During the past 50 years, most schools of Qinqiang have tended to decline and gradually be replaced by Central Qinqiang.

The heyday of Qinqiang was in the Qianlong period (1736-1795), during which time Qinqiang troupes could be found in many areas all over the country. In Xi'an alone there were 36 Qinqiang performing troupes, such as the Baofu Troupe (保符班), the Jiangdong Troupe (江东班), the Shuangzhai Troupe (双寨班) and the Jinxiu Troupe (锦绣班), to name just a few.

Artistic Characteristics of Qinqiang Opera

Qinqiang Opera Tunes and Music

The most striking characteristics of Qinqiang are its loud and vehement singing style and its strong and rapid rhythm. The painted face characters, in particular, sing so loudly and hit such extremely high notes that local people call their singing style "loud and explosive," and people from outside Shaanxi who are not familiar with this operatic form would jokingly call it "the deafening, straining and frightening opera."

Qinqiang tunes are divided into *ban lu* (板路, clapper tunes) and *cai qiang* (彩腔, trills), and for each there are "joyous tones" (*huan yin*, 欢音) and "sad tones" (*ku yin*, 苦音) characterizing a pleasant mood and a melancholy mood, respectively, of which the sad tones may best represent the features of Qinqiang opera. As regards clapper tunes, there are six basic clapping styles, namely two-six clappers, slow clappers, arrow clappers, substitute clappers, pitch clappers and roll clappers. Trills are high-pitched tunes that usually stand for strong emotions quirky twists of plot. Clapper tunes are sung in chest voice and trills in falsetto. In the case of most Qinqiang opera roles, including *xu sheng* (old male roles with a beard), *qing yi, lao sheng, lao dan* and "painted face" roles, singing represents a significant part of their performance, which is why singing Qinqiang opera is popularly called "singing *luan tan*," and before the Qing Dynasty, Qinqiang was indeed called "Xi'an *luan tan.*" Some *luan tan* passages sung by male characters may extend to dozens of lines, such as those in *The White-faced Traitor Minister Forcing the Emperor to Abdicate* (*bai bi gong*,《白逼宫》), *Expedition to Hedong Area*(*xia he dong*,《下河东》) and *Beheading Li Guang* (*zhan li guang*《斩李广》). The tunes composed for painted face characters are extremely high-pitched and difficult, and those able to sing well tend to be famous Qinqiang performers. There are six types of fixed melodies in Qinqiang opera, namely those played by string instruments, by the *suona*, by the *haidi* (a kind of flute), by the *sheng* and by the pipe as well as melodies borrowed from Kunqu opera and sets of fixed melodies, with the first two (those played by stringed instruments and those played by *suona*) being the main types of Qinqiang fixed melodies. The musical band may play according to two different "settings": the "quiet setting," which relies mainly on the *banhu* fiddle, with support from the flute, the three-string fiddle, the moon zither and the trumpet; and the "dynamic setting," which mostly relies on percussion instruments — such as finger clappers, the plain drum, the rough drum, the war drum, the hook gong and the hand gong — and the *shuishui* zither.[1]

---

[1] http://english.chinese.cn/chineseculture/article/2011-07/15/content_294673.htm.

Role Categories and Performance of Qinqiang Opera

Qinqiang opera has its particular tradition of role categories, including the *sheng*, *dan*, *jing* and *chou*, and as in other traditional Chinese operas, there are subdivisions under each category. Traditionally, thirteen performers may form a troupe: four males, six females, two painted faces and one clown, and these performers are further divided into three classes. The "first-class" roles are the first-class bearded male roles, the *zheng dan*, the painted faces and the *xiao dan*; the "second-class roles" are the *xiao sheng*, the second-class beards, the second-class painted faces and the clowns; all other roles are third-class roles. The best performers in each class of roles may become leading roles, and troupes with sound financial standing could pay high prices to recruit famous

Characters of Qinqiang opera

performers. The most versatile performers can play various roles in all kinds of plays. Qinqiang performers are also skilled at various postures and motions; special shows can include horse riding, fire breathing, a boatman show, and capture and fall feats. Indeed, this opera is famous for its wonderful acts and sideshows, which will be touched upon in detail in a separate section of this chapter.

Lyrical Structure of Qinqiang Opera

Qinqiang opera lyrics are composed of lines with a fixed number of characters, the most common being seven-character or ten-character lines, making the entire play a neatly-patterned blank verse of which each line contains seven or ten characters. The musical tunes accompanying these patterns are, on the other hand, in changing metric-type style (板式变化体), with the metric types changing from an unfixed beat (*san ban*) to a slow beat (*man ban*), on to a median beat, and finally, a fast beat. These metric types follow in proper sequence order, so that performers may sing seven- or ten-character lines with the above metric types, thus gradually unfolding the dramatic plot.

Traditional Sideshows of Qinqiang Opera

Fire Spitting

Fire spitting (*chui huo*, 吹火), or fire breathing (*pen huo*, 喷火), is a feat often found in plays with monsters, devils and ghosts. An example of this is the character Li Huiniang's use of this feat in the Qinqiang play *Touring West Lake – Saving Pei the Scholar* (《游西湖·救裴生》). Traditionally, performers first wrap fine rosin powder with long-fiber paper into a small paper bag, with a small opening, that can be held in the mouth. During the show, the performer spits the rosin powder onto the torch, which immediately bursts into flame and creates a fireball.

Dangerous as it may seem, performers often assume various postures when performing fire spitting on stage, and with different spitting techniques, the flames may take on different shapes. The fire-spitting technique employed in Qinqiang opera is indeed very unique, and many other genres of traditional opera acquired the technique from Qinqiang.

Lamp Holding

Balancing a burning oil lamp on his head, the performer executes various actions. Chang Tianbao, a clown character in the play *Three Successful Candidates to the Imperial Examination* (*san jin shi*, 《三进士》), carries an oil lamp on his head as a punishment for gambling

Fire spitting (*chui huo*), a traditional Qinqiang opera sideshow

Lamp holding (*ding deng*), a traditional Qinqiang opera sideshow

inflicted by his wife. The performer playing this role must be good at assuming all kinds of postures and doing all kinds of activities while holding the lamp, and he has to ensure the lamp does not fall down, the oil does not spill out, and the lamp keeps burning. It is a veritable test of the performer's sense of balance.

Bowl Smashing

Bowl smashing is an act used to beat ghosts, usually seen in plays performed during temple fairs. It is also performed by painted face roles and bearded male roles, such as the celestial official in *Sacrificing to the Deities on the Stage* (*da tai,*《打台》) and Sun Wuzi in *The Taihe Castle* (*tai he cheng,*《太和城》). The performer throws a bowl in the air, spinning, and then sends another bowl smashing into it, so that

Stilt-walking   Playing with teeth

both bowls break into pieces in mid-air. Performers use a variety of bowl smashing techniques to create various visual effects.

Lamp Whipping

This is a trick played by painted face and clown roles of Qinqiang opera. The performer first prepares paper flowers and ties them to the end of his whips. During the performance, a pair of oil lamps is hanging over the stage; to the beat of percussion instruments, he crosses the whips in front of himself, and whips the oil lamps repeatedly, so that the stage flickers with sparks of fire. The oil lamp near the performer becomes brighter when the lamp wick is whipped off, in order for the audience to see the expressions on the performer's face and in his eyes. The performer therefore needs great skill to carry out this act, as all movements must be made on time and with good coordination. Nowadays, oil lamps are no longer used to light up the stage, and this trick is not part of the Qinqiang sideshow repertoire any more.

Stilt-Walking

This trick is played by *dan* roles of Qinqiang opera. The wooden stilts are small and pointed, around three inches long, and wrapped with small, embroidered shoes. The performer has to have the stilts and shoes attached

Stilt-walking

to her shoes, and she must walk on the stage with two toes, raising her heels very high. The difficult part of this trick is that the performer is not only required to walk beautifully and gracefully, but sometimes has to demonstrate her mastery of various difficult moves.

Teeth Tricks

Teeth tricks are played by *mao jing* roles (毛净, these are either celestial gods or people with deformities; these roles have exaggerated shapes, and performers in this line of business must be especially good at movements and postures) of Qinqiang opera, as well as of other related local operas. These tricks include that of "clenching teeth" and that of "playing with teeth."

Clenching teeth, or grinding teeth, is a trick often used by painted face roles to show their strong hatred. The performer clenches his teeth and grinds them loudly. The difficult part of this trick is that the grinding sound must be loud and carry far away while not being unpleasant to the ear; the performer must therefore have skillful control over his teeth movements.

Playing with teeth involves the tongue's maneuvering of 2-4 pig teeth, which are made heavy and connected with a thread. The performer not only plays various tricks with the pig teeth, but also sings and recites clearly while holding the teeth in his mouth.

CHAPTER VI
Exquisite and Sophisticated Sichuan Opera: Among the Best of the World

Sichuan opera is a brilliant pearl in the treasure house of traditional Chinese opera. It enjoys a long history and has an outstanding repertoire of plays, as well as prolific melodies and exquisite performing art. Sichuan opera is a folk art extremely popular in the southwestern part of China, including Sichuan, Yunnan and Guizhou provinces, and it is also a cultural form characteristic of Sichuan. Chengdu, the capital of Sichuan Province, has long been home to traditional opera, and as early as the Tang Dynasty, there was a saying that "operas in the Sichuan area are the best in the world." During Emperor Qianlong's reign in the Qing Dynasty, the local opera, known as *che deng xi* (车灯戏 "lantern opera") began to assimilate tunes from other geographical areas, including Suzhou, Jiangxi, Anhui, Hubei, Shaanxi and Gansu, and thus a new "Sichuan opera" was formed, integrating high-pitched tunes, Huqin tunes, Kun tunes, lantern opera and *tanxi* (another form of local Sichuan opera) and sung in Sichuan dialect. High-pitched tunes include a great number of melodies and beautiful tunes, and particularly characterize this local opera, of which they represent the most central component. There are a number of

different forms of musical accompaniment in Sichuan opera, including collar resonance, combined resonance, chorus, vocal accompaniment and instrumental accompaniment, which give enduring appeal to the plays. The lyrics of Sichuan opera feature lively and humorous language, and they draw a particular charm from local color; they are full of life, and highly appreciated by the local audience. There are several hundred plays of Sichuan opera still performed on stage today. This operatic form is also well known for its unique sideshows including face changing, fire breathing and water sleeves, and its easy-going stylized movements are guaranteed to be a feast for the eyes. Sichuan opera is popular among people throughout the country and has spread all over the world.

The History of Sichuan Opera

The origins of Sichuan opera can be dated back to pre-Qin days or even earlier times, and its overall structure was founded on the basis of the entertainment wrestling and acrobatics of the post-Han age. In the well-known article of the Warring States Period "Song Yu's Reply to King of Chu's Questions" (《宋玉对楚王问》), one reads that "they are folk singers and dancers, and there are several thousand of them in the country." In this passage, the performers are referred to as "*xia li ba ren*" (下里巴人) in Chinese. This is a derogatory term, referring to all folk singers and dancers in the Sichuan area, and designating performers of lowbrow artistic forms. According to *Extensive Records of the Taiping Era* (*tai ping guang ji*, 《太平广记》), a fictional history edited by Li Fang (李昉) of the Song Dynasty, and the *Collection of Barnyard Grass History* (*bai shi hui bian*, 《稗史汇编》), compiled by Wang Qi (王圻) of the Ming Dynasty, there were operas played in the Sichuan area, such as the play *Bullfight* (《斗牛》), ever since Li Bing was the senior provincial official of Sichuan in the Qin Dynasty during the third century BC. During the Three Kingdoms Period (220-265 AD), the first satirical comedy *Anger and Contention* (*fen zheng*, 《忿争》) was performed on stage in the Sichuan area, and it is thus regarded as the earliest Sichuan opera comedy. From the Tang Dynasty till the Five Dynasties Period

Sichuan opera stage performance

(618-947), *za ju* was a popular operatic form in China, and it was during this period that Sichuan opera thrived, giving rise to the saying that "operas in the Sichuan area are the best in the world." During the late Ming and early Qing dynasties, as a result of massacres as well as years of turmoil after the Manchu invasion, the population of Sichuan fell sharply, requiring a massive resettlement of people from other provinces including Hunan, Hubei and Guangdong provinces, which is historically known as "Huguang people filling Sichuan" (湖广填四川).[1] The immigrants from

---

[1] http://en.wikipedia.org/wiki/Sichuan.

Sichuan opera performance

Sichuan opera performance

other provinces brought their own folk operas and operatic tunes to Sichuan, and Sichuan opera gradually took shape, taking the local lantern opera as its basis, but also integrating high-pitched tunes, Kun tunes, Huqin tunes and *tan* tunes; the result featured a strong blend of Sichuan dialect and local culture, along with artistic elements of folk music, singing and dancing.

Artistic Characteristics of Sichuan Opera

Sichuan Opera Tunes and Music

As mentioned above, Sichuan opera originated from the local lantern opera of the Sichuan area, while the tunes of Sichuan opera took shape by integrating the operatic tunes of other operas as well as folk songs from other geographical areas.

Sichuan Kunqu (*chuan kun* 川昆) evolved from Kunqu of the Jiangsu area (or *su kun* 苏昆), which spread into Sichuan during the late Ming Dynasty. After the beginning of the Qing Dynasty, a huge number of people resettled in Sichuan, among whom many imperial officials and other personalities who were fond of Kunqu opera, and who thus brought their family troupes to Sichuan. In Sichuan, the original melodies of the Kun tunes remained, but in order to better agree with the local audience, the lines began to be sung and spoken in Sichuan dialect, hence the Sichuan Kunqu. Besides, Kun tunes were integrated with other tunes including high-pitched tunes, Huqin tunes and *tan* tunes, and were performed in various combinations of operatic tunes; sometimes, the integration would also take the form of *Kun touzi* (literally "Kunqu as the lead"), meaning the play would be performed by combining the fixed melodies of Kunqu opera with other operatic tunes. Meanwhile, *chuiqiang* (吹腔 "blowing tunes"), a singing style of Anhui opera, was also integrated into the Kun tunes. Thus Kunqu evolved into an operatic tune with special Sichuan characteristics, Sichuan Kunqu, by integrating its own tunes with the local dialects, folk music and percussions of Sichuan opera.

High-pitched tunes (*gaoqiang* 高腔), an extremely free singing style devoid of musical accompaniment, are particularly representative of Sichuan opera. Singers sing the loud and vehement high-pitched tunes to the beats of clappers and other percussion instruments, and there are vocal accompaniments. Loud drums and gongs are used as percussion instruments throughout the entire melodies, so that the singing, beats and vocal accompaniments are well coordinated, which creates a very rich and vibrant stage atmosphere.

Huqin tunes (*huqin qiang*, 胡琴腔) are also known as "*si xian zi*" (丝弦子, silk strings) because the *huqin*, a two-string instrument, is the main

CHAPTER VI

Sichuan opera water sleeves performance

instrument for musical accompaniment. They evolved from Anhui tunes and Han tunes, and assimilated elements from the Hanzhong *erhuang* (汉中二簧) of Shaanxi. While they include both *xipi* and *erhuang* types of music, they display unique characteristics in terms of tunes, beats and interludes, and are sung in Sichuan dialects.

Tanxi tunes (弹戏), also known as "Sichuan *bangzi*" (川梆子) or "*gai banzi*" (盖板子), are a variant of Qinqiang opera in Sichuan. Qinqiang spread into Sichuan early after it took shape, and throughout its development in Sichuan, it adapted itself to suit local aesthetics — recitation notably switched from the Shaanxi dialect to the Sichuan dialect — and gradually integrated with Huqin tunes, high-pitched tunes

and other tunes in Sichuan opera, or became a part of performance in other tunes. Many Sichuan opera plays are primarily based on *tanxi* tunes, while integrating Huqin tunes and lantern tunes.

Lantern tunes (*deng diao* 灯调) originated in the folk music, singing and dancing performed at local lantern fairs, a Sichuanese tradition. They are mostly folk ditties accompanied by the *pang tong tong* (胖筒筒), a musical instrument; consequently, lantern tunes are also known as "*pang tong tong.*" In their development, these tunes assimilated the traditions of northern and southern folk melodies, and became a regular performance in lantern fairs during the Lantern Festival. The melodies of lantern tunes are usually short, with clear rhythms and clean rhymes, so that the tunes sound quite lively, and they are often used with witty and humorous comedies.

Sichuan opera music is quite special in its style, featuring extraordinary percussion music; the gong and drum components of Sichuan opera are indeed the most outstanding among all traditional Chinese operas, with their loud sound, clear and vibrant rhythms and special tones. Sichuan opera percussion music includes very diversified melodies and can be used with all the tunes mentioned above, and right on the beat of the singing, recitation, acting and acrobatic fighting of performers. Wind also plays a fundamental role; there are as many fixed melodies for the *suona* as for gongs and drums. In Sichuan opera, string music also features the *huqin* and the bamboo flute, and some fixed melodies are played with these instruments. Other instruments include the "zigzag flute" in the case of Sichuan Kunqu tunes, the small *huqin* for huqin tunes, the *gai ban* (盖板) for *tanxi* tunes and the *"mi hu zi"* (迷胡子) for lantern tunes. In a word, the music of Sichuan opera is quite diverse in terms of artistic styles.

Facial Make-up and Face Changing

Facial make-up is an integral part of the performance of Sichuan opera, and it is regarded as a gem of this special operatic art, jointly created and carried forward by generations of Sichuan opera performers.

Before the show, performers of Sichuan opera paint various designs on their faces with different colors, as a means of showing each character's social status, appearance and personalities. Traditionally there was no professional facial painter in Sichuan opera troupes, so that performers had to paint the facial make-up by themselves. This way the individual performer could create his own facial make-up according to his own facial features, as long as it suited the basic characteristics of the role he played, so as to attract the attention of the audience. Therefore, Sichuan opera is quite unique among traditional Chinese local operas for its individuality and diversity.

The colors used for facial make-up constitute a character's most important distinctive sign in Sichuan opera, and the principles followed in the use of different colors are based on traditional Chinese beliefs and on the psychological habits of the Chinese audience. For example, the color red is used to represent characters with good faith, virtue and patriotism, like Guan Yu and Jiang Wei; the color black is used to represent upright and selfless characters, such as Bao Zheng, and the color white is used to represent cruel and sinister characters, like Cao Cao.

With the above basic principles of color usage, performers of Sichuan opera paint designs with symbolic moral meanings on their faces to show the personalities of specific characters in the plays. Everyone's moral judgment — the playwrights' as well as the audience's — regarding each

Sichuan opera water sleeves performance

Sichuan opera masks

Sichuan opera fire spitting

Face changing, a unique sideshow of Sichuan opera

Sichuan opera performance

character can thus be immediately understood from the various facial designs. For example, such designs as a brush rack in the form of the Chinese character 山 (mountain), a vermillion brush, the character 寿 (longevity), a crescent or a sun can be painted on Bao Zheng's black face to symbolize his decency and integrity. On the red face of Guan Yu, such designs as bushy eyebrows, three incense sticks or the character 品 (character) can be painted to symbolize his faith, bravery and credibility.

Characterization through the facial painting of animal designs is another major feature of Sichuan opera. For example, Ma Jun, a legendary heroic figure, is nicknamed "Jade Butterfly" by people; as a result, a colorful butterfly is painted on the face of the actor playing the part of this character. In the same way, a duck with spread wings is painted on the face of whoever plays the character known as the "Green Duck Taoist," and a greenish blue coiled snake over that of the performer playing the part of a snake spirit.

Another way of characterizing through facial make-up is to paint

Chinese calligraphy on the actor's face, along with other patterns. This was a method preferred by performers of Sichuan opera before the 1950s.

However, during a Sichuan opera performance, the facial make-up sometimes changes following plot development, and the alteration of the characters' psychological state. In order to proceed to these changes, the performers invented various face-changing tricks, including face rubbing, face spitting, and face tearing. These tricks are all performed extremely quickly on stage during the performance without being perceived by the audience, so as to create an extraordinary effect on the senses.

The earlier facial make-up mostly relied on paper masks. Later, it evolved into facial make-up painted on rough straw paper, which was worn by the performers layer upon layer beforehand and was then peeled off, layer after layer, during the performance, under the camouflage of pyrotechnics or behind an unfolded fan. After the founding of the People's Republic of China in 1949, face-changing tricks experienced a rapid development, and now that facial make-up is made of silk, Sichuan opera performers may use these tricks more easily and to better effect.

As mentioned above, there are three ways to carry out face-changing in Sichuan opera, namely face rubbing, face spitting and face tearing.

Face rubbing is a technique in which a performer uses cosmetic paints to draw special designs on his face; during the performance, the colors of his facial make-up will change whenever he rubs his face. If there is a

Sichuan opera performance

Face changing, a unique sideshow of Sichuan opera

need to change his entire facial make-up, he applies the make-up on his forehead or on his eyebrows, and if he just needs to change the lower part of the facial make-up, the paints are applied on his cheeks or nose. The character Xu Xian in *The Tale of the White Snake* (*bai she zhuan*《白蛇传》) changes his facial make-up in this way.

Face spitting is a technique in which the performer puts a certain amount of cosmetic powder, of golden, silver or black color, in a special container; during the performance, he approaches the container and spits the powder so that his face is sprayed with the powder. The performer must close his eyes and mouth and stop breathing for a short while after spitting the powder. In the play *Catching Zidu Alive* (*huo zhuo zi du*, 《活捉子都》), the cosmetic powder is put in a wine cup, but in most cases it is placed inside a small box and put on the floor of the stage. With a dancing movement like that of kissing the ground, the performer brings his face near the box and spits the powder.

Face tearing is the most complicated technique of the three. Before the performance, the facial make-up is painted on several sheets of silk, each of which is tied to a silk thread on one end and then glued on the performer's face layer upon layer. The other end of each silk thread is attached to a hidden spot on the performer's costume (such as his waistband), enabling him to tear his "faces" easily. Following developments in the dramatic plot, the facial make-up can be torn off layer after layer under the camouflage of a dancing movement. The bowl child in the play *The Tale of the White Snake*, for example, may change faces as many as seven or eight times, each of which is a different color, in this way. Other examples include that of the thief in *The Old Main Building* (*jiu zheng lou*, 《旧正楼》) and Nie Long in *The Beach of Mother-Waiting* (*wang niang tan*, 《望娘滩》). This is the most difficult face-changing technique, because it requires a skillful use of glue, for fear that the silk would be glued together too strongly to be torn off, or that all the silk sheets would be torn off at once. The performer must also perform the movement very skillfully under the camouflage of deceptive movements for the audience not to see the trick.

Status and Development of Sichuan Opera

Extremely valuable for the research of the culture, art, history and folk customs of the Sichuan area, Sichuan opera has a unique status in China's operatic history and in the history of Sichuanese cultural development. Thanks to China's central government concern for the protection of intangible cultural heritage, on May 20, 2006, the incorporation of Sichuan opera into the first List of Intangible Cultural Heritage was approved by the State Council of the People's Republic of China. On June 8, 2007, the Sichuan Opera School was also awarded the first Cultural Heritage Day Award by the Ministry of Culture.

CHAPTER VII
Distinctive and Graceful Cantonese Opera:
A Southern Chinese Opera in Cantonese

A local opera performed by people of the Han ethnic group, Cantonese opera was formerly called *da xi* (大戏, literally "big opera") or "Guangdong *da xi*" (广东大戏). It is rooted in *nanxi*, a southern drama of the late Song Dynasty, and emerged in Guangdong and Guangxi during Emperor Jiajing's reign in the Ming Dynasty (1522-1566). Cantonese opera is a performance art integrating singing, recitation, acting and acrobatic fighting, characterized by elegant musical accompaniment and costumes, and stylized movements. Each role category in Cantonese opera includes particular costumes and a specific dressing style. While it was originally sung in the dialect of the Central Plains, known as the "official language of the operatic theatre," toward the end of the Qing Dynasty the revolutionaries made Cantonese opera a means to advocate revolution against the Qing government, and therefore changed the language to Cantonese to make it more easily understood by local people. On May 20, 2006, Cantonese opera was included among the 518 items of the first national list of Intangible

Cultural Heritage, with the approval of the State Council. On September 30, 2009, the United Nations Educational, Scientific and Cultural Organization (UNESCO) approved the incorporation of Cantonese opera into the Representative List of the Intangible Cultural Heritage of Humanity.

The History of Cantonese Opera

Also known as *da xi* (literally "big opera") or "Guangdong *da xi*", Cantonese opera is one of the major operatic forms of South China. It took shape by integrating Haiyan tunes, Yiyang tunes, Kunshan tunes and *bangzi*, which had all spread to Guangdong during the Ming and Qing dynasties, and assimilating artistic elements from the folk music sung by the inhabitants of the Pearl River Delta. Musically, it is mainly based on *bangzi* (*xipi* in Peking opera) and *erhuang*. It is popular in Guangdong, Guangxi, Taiwan, Hong Kong and Macao, and Cantonese opera performances can be seen in areas inhabited by Cantonese communities all over the world, including Singapore, Malaysia, Vietnam, Myanmar, Cambodia, the Philippines, Indonesia, Australia, the United States, Canada, Mexico, Cuba and other Latin American countries.

While it evolved from *nanxi* (southern drama), Cantonese opera was originally sung in the dialect of the Central Plains, known as the "official language of the operatic theatre." However, at the end of the Qing Dynasty, the revolutionaries made Cantonese opera a means to advocate revolution against Qing government rule, and therefore changed the language to Cantonese to make it more easily understood by local people.

In the fifth year of Emperor Yongzheng's reign in the Qing Dynasty, Zhang Wu, a famous performer from Beijing, fled in disguise to

Guangdong. He eventually settled in the town of Foshan and made a living by teaching Peking opera and Kunqu opera to the so-called "red-boat performers" (meaning performers of Cantonese opera, since at that time they

Cantonese opera performance

took red boats as a means of transportation), and founded the Qionghua Operatic Association (琼花会馆), the earliest theatrical organization of Cantonese opera; Foshan is thus regarded as the hometown of Cantonese opera. At that time, there were many folk festivals involving god shrines in Foshan, and whenever such festivals took place, Cantonese opera performances would follow. Cantonese opera was thus extremely popular, which can be seen from some literary works of the time.

Although the name "Cantonese opera" did not appear until Emperor Guangxu's reign, it can be dated back to 400 years before, during the mid-Ming Dynasty.

During the Ming Dynasty, Yiyang tunes of the southern tradition were already very popular in Guangdong, and Kunshan operatic troupes from Jiangsu, Anhui, Jiangxi and Hunan often came to perform in the Guangdong area. According to *The History of Cantonese Opera* (《粤

Cantonese opera

剧史》), there was a *hua dan* actress living in Guangdong, whose name was Zhang Qiao, and who was born into a family of performers in Nanhai. Zhang's ancestral town was Suzhou but she was born in Guangdong, and she was recorded as a female performer of Kun tunes because her mother was a performer of Kunqu opera. From this we can see that performers from various geographical areas began to settle in Guangdong at that time. Influenced by them, people in Guangdong began to learn performing operas, but at that time, operatic performance was yet to gain the appreciation of conservative people in Guangdong, and families with a higher social status forbade their members to become performers. Later, performing troupes mainly consisting of local people grew more common in the area, and later still, performing troupes appeared that consisted solely of local people. To differentiate these performing troupes, the former were called "*wai jiang ban* (外江班, literally "troupes of performers from the other side of the river") and the latter were called *ben di ban* (本地班, "troupes of local performers").

Foshan was the earliest congregation center for *bendi ban*. In 1658 (the fifteenth year of Emperor Shunzhi's reign in the Qing Dynasty), the Huafeng Operatic Stage (华封戏台) was built in front of Lingyingci (灵应祠) Ancestral Temple, and included all necessary props. During the 1661-1722 period (Emperor Kangxi's reign) the name of the stage was changed to Wanfu Operatic Stage (万福台). Today, it remains the most exquisite

Cantonese opera

antique operatic stage in Guangdong Province, and the largest one in the entire area south of the Five Ridges; it has witnessed the development of Cantonese opera for the past several hundred years. The stage is divided into two parts, the front stage and the backstage. Wooden carvings painted golden decorated the front stage, and constituted a wonderful background for the performance. The Wanfu Operatic Stage adopted arch structures, so as to create excellent sound effects.

During Emperor Yongzheng's reign (1722-1735), *tu you* (土优, local performers) and *tu ban* (土班, local performing troupes) were commonly seen in the city of Guangzhou. Historical literature shows that besides Kunqu opera, Cantonese tunes were quite popular and well accepted in the area during this time. Under Emperor Qianlong's reign (1735-1795), the Guangdong area experienced prolonged peace, security

蘇容珍 周淑華 曹啟興 周春華 周影華
Susan So　Sandra Young　Raymond Cao　Donna Tan　Vicky Zhou

Cantonese opera

and prosperity. Foshan, in particular, was a center of business activities, and business people had more demands for entertainment, so that over a hundred performing troupes from outside Guangdong, including Jiangxi, Hunan, Anhui and Jiangsu, traveled there to perform. In 1759 (the 24th year of Emperor Qianlong's reign) these performing troupes jointly established the Association of Operatic Performing Troupes from Outside Guangdong Province (粤省外江梨园会馆) in Guangzhou, while local performing troupes established the Qionghua Association (琼花会馆), in Foshan. In the less developed areas in the western part of

Guangdong Province, namely Gaozhou, Leizhou, Lianzhou and Qiongzhou prefectures, operatic performances were also very popular, and performing operas to celebrate the birthdays of gods had become a folk custom in the area.

Cantonese opera

In the year 1854 (the fourth year of Emperor Xianfeng's reign), in response to the Taiping Rebellion, Li Wenmao, a Cantonese opera performer, led some operatic performers from Foshan in a rebellion against the Qing government, and divided them into three military troops. The Qing government thus killed many performers, destroyed the Qionghua Association and banned Cantonese opera for as long as 15 years. During this time, some Cantonese opera performers fled to other provinces or even to overseas, occasionally joining operatic troupes from outside the province and performing other local operas, thus facilitating the integration between the *bangzi* and *erhuang* operatic styles. In 1861 (the 11th year of Emperor Xianfeng's reign), Li Wenmao and Chen Kai were defeated and killed, and the ban on Cantonese opera was loosened, providing an opportunity for the thriving of local troupes. In 1870 (the ninth year of Emperor Tongzhi's reign), Feng Guangwei and others from Gaoyao County of Guangdong Province submitted a written request to the county magistrate to allow nighttime operatic performances; permission was granted, an evidence that the ban was lifted during this period of time.

Meanwhile, a huge number of Chinese workmen were deluded into doing extremely heavy labor work overseas, and Cantonese opera was thus spread outside China. In Jack Chen's *Chinese in America* (《美国华人史》) he wrote that "[at that time] shows became a regular feature of San Francisco entertainment and paved the way for the Hook Took Tong, a Chinese theatrical troupe with 123 performers that opened with a program of Cantonese opera at the American Theatre (October 18, 1852). This was so successful that the troupe imported its own theatre building from China, and erected it in Chinatown by the end of the year." Besides, a large number of Chinese residents gone to settle in Vietnam, Singapore, Indonesia and other countries were Cantonese; Cantonese opera being very popular among them, performing troupes also appeared in those countries. In the 1870s, the translation in Javanese of such Cantonese opera plays as *Xue Rengui* (《薛仁贵》), *Yang Zhongbao* (《杨忠保》), *Di Qing* (《狄青》) and *A Dignified Lady* (*gui furen*,《贵夫人》) were published, and later the Malay translation of the play *Emperor Qianlong Visiting Jiangnan* (*Qianlong jun you jiang nan*《乾隆君游江南》) was also published.

After the Qing government ban on Cantonese opera was lifted,

Cantonese opera

Cantonese opera

the performing style of troupes of local performers changed a lot; they assimilated the *erhuang* style into their tunes, and sang *bangzi, erhuang* and other major tunes in their performance. At that time, there were ten role categories in Cantonese opera, namely *wu sheng* (武生), *zheng sheng* (正生), *xiao sheng, xiao wu* (小武), *zong sheng* (总生), *gong jiao* (公脚), *zheng dan, hua dan, jing* and *chou*. Later, the efforts of Kuang Xinhua, Du Jiao Ying, Lin Zhi and others led to the rebirth of Cantonese opera, and a new union of performers, the Bahe Association (八和会馆), was established. In the beginning of the 20th century, Chinese intellectuals began to promote national reform in all local operas. In 1898 (the 24th year of Emperor Guangxu's reign), the ten-day supplement of *China*, a daily newspaper launched by Sun Yat-sen in Hong Kong, opened a special section called "*gu chui lu*" (鼓吹录, literally "Drums of Advocacy"), in which some journalists including Yang Xiao'ou and Huang Luyi wrote operatic ballads to satirize the current affairs of the time, to which other Guangzhou and Hong Kong newspapers responded actively. In 1903 (the 29th year of Emperor Guangxu's reign), an operatic play review attacked the script for being "pedant," claiming that the plays of the time could not arouse the enthusiasm of Chinese people about national reform. After that, an increasing number of plays were written and performed to reflect the current state of society.

Around the period of the Xinhai Revolution, some senior performers of Cantonese opera, including Jin Shanbing and Zhu Cibo, began the campaign to reform Cantonese opera. As a result of this reform, in 1905 Xiyuan (literally "opera court") Theatre was established in Guangzhou. This event changed the performing style of Cantonese opera in several ways. Previously, opera performances took place on temporary outdoor stages (where performers had to sing with a high-pitched voice in order to be heard by the audience), and performers had to roam from one place to another. Whereas after the opera court was established, performers could perform indoors, and therefore sing with softer voices; besides, since the audience came to see the performance at a fixed location, the performers had to make sure they could attract the public. It was during this time that Zhu Cibo, who was a fresh performer at that time, performed the play *Baoyu Wailing* (*Baoyu ku ling*, 《宝玉哭灵》) in a soft voice, which proved a great success. Singing softly thus became the fashion of the time.

In the 1950s, shortly after the founding of the People's Republic of China, people in Cantonese opera circles made active efforts to renovate the art form and create outstanding plays, to carry forward the fine tradition of Cantonese opera while reforming this operatic form overall, and trained a number of fresh performers. The Guangdong Cantonese Opera Troupe was established in 1959, and the Guangdong Cantonese Opera School and its Zhanjiang Branch were established in 1950 and

Typical Cantonese opera body moves

Distinctive and Graceful Cantonese Opera: A Southern Chinese Opera in Cantonese

Cantonese opera performance

1962, respectively. Thus for the first time in the history of Cantonese opera there were special schools to train Cantonese opera performers.

Artistic Characteristics of Cantonese Opera

Performance of Cantonese Opera

The Cantonese opera performance, like that of other traditional Chinese operas, consists of singing, body movements, recitation and acrobatic fighting. Singing requires the performer to adopt different styles according to different role categories, which includes singing in a soft voice and singing in falsetto. Singing in a soft voice actually means singing in chest voice, which is usually required for male roles, like the *xiao sheng*. Falsetto is an octave above the chest voice, and it is usually adopted to impersonate female characters. Besides, Cantonese opera assimilated particular tunes and features from different places, such as tunes from Fujian or other local folk music.

Body movements include hand gestures, footwork, body positions, eye movements, body postures, "water sleeves," plume movements and beard movements, symbolic movements and traditional skills. Recitation involves presenting the plot and the characters' emotions by reciting the lines of the play. Acrobatic fighting includes moving water sleeves" and "water hair," playing with various weapons, waving flags, etc.

Cantonese Opera Tunes and Music

In the early 18th century, some *waijiang ban* brought Yiyang tunes and Kunshan tunes to Guangdong Province, and while local performing troupes were already found in the area before the Taiping Rebellion, their tunes still featured *bangzi*. After the decline of Kunqu opera, Cantonese opera began to feature *xipi* and *erhuang* as its major tunes, an influence of Anhui operatic troupes. After the Xinhai Revolution, the Cantonese opera reform started with the language of the opera — as mentioned above, it was changed from the mandarin "official language" into Cantonese, which was called "*xin qiang*" (new tunes). During the Anti-Japanese War(1937-1945), many senior performers of Cantonese opera begar in-depth studies of the Cantonese operatic tunes and developed

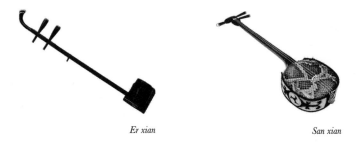

Er xian   *San xian*

Yue qin   Horizontal and vertical bamboo flutes

their own tunes. Thus Cantonese opera began to feature various tunes with distinct styles.

There are three categories of tunes and music of Cantonese opera: the beat-and-tune style (*ban qiang ti*), the fixed-melody style (*qu pai ti*) and the psalm style (*shi zan ti*,诗赞体), which are rooted in the development of traditional Chinese opera and of Cantonese opera in particular. The psalm style is also called "talking-and-singing style" (*shuo changti*, 说唱体). The local operatic music of Guangdong also features such folk music traditions as those of *nan yin* (南音), *mu yu* (木鱼), *long zhou* (龙舟), *ban yan* (板眼) and *yue o* (粤讴). Due to the special features of Cantonese dialects, the talking and singing style and tunes are quite different from those in the northern areas of China.

The beat-and-tune style (*ban qiang ti*) is the basic feature of

Cantonese opera performance

Cantonese opera. Because it consists of *bangzi* and *erhuang*, it is popularly known as "*banghuang,*" somewhat similarly to the *pihuang* (皮黄) of Peking opera. Therefore, Cantonese opera is by definition an operatic form integrating both the northern and southern styles — namely the *erhuan* tunes from southern operas and the *pihuang* tunes from northern operas. The beat-and-tune style of Cantonese opera was brought from outside Guangdong Province. It is an integration of talking and singing tunes from local music traditions with clapper beats, in which the tunes change according to different metrics, and hence corresponds to a "changing metril-type style" (板式变化体).

The fundamental difference between the above three styles of operatic tunes is that there is no fixed melody in beat-and-tune style or in psalm style. The melodies of these tunes are determined by the lyrics, and different melodies can be used with different lyrics, even in the case of a same metril pattern. For the fixed-melody style, on the other hand, different lyrics are used with the fixed melodies, of which the major tones always remain unchanged.

Stylized Movements of Cantonese Opera

As in the case of all other local operas in China, the ability to perform highly stylized movements and postures constitutes one of the basic skills of a Chinese opera performer. These stylized movements and postures have been systemized and are highly symbolic, so as to present the personalities and emotions of characters along with plot development. In the case of Cantonese opera, there are a whole set of basic body postures and movements, and like in other operatic forms, different movements are used for different role categories. For example, the walking style of *xiao sheng* (young males) roles is the "T-step," in which the feet form the shape of a "T, in order to express an air of dignity and respectability. *Hua dan* (vivacious young females) roles, on the other hand, must walk in a lively and relaxed fashion, so as to represent the character's vivacity. And naturally, for each subdivision of all other categories, there is also a whole set of routinized postures and movements. These stylized movements and postures are also used to represent emotions as well as all kinds of activities on behalf of the characters in the development of the plot.

Music Instruments and Accompaniment of Cantonese Opera

Originally, musical instruments were used for the musical accompaniment of Cantonese opera — mostly wind and string instruments, and some simple percussion instruments. After the ban on Cantonese opera was lifted, the *bangzi* (clapper) was added to the band. When Cantonese opera became more mature, over 40 music instruments began to be used for musical accompaniment: winds, plucked and bowed strings, and percussion instruments. Following the reform of Cantonese

Cantonese opera performance

Cantonese opera

opera, a number of Western instruments, including the saxophone and the violin, started to be used in Cantonese opera to create wonderful sound effects on stage.

Status and Development of Cantonese Opera

Since the Chinese economic reform, most traditions suppressed during the "cultural revolution" of 1966-1976 have experienced a rebirth, among which that of Cantonese opera. In the 20 years following the end of the "cultural revolution", many performing troupes of Cantonese opera were established in the Chinese mainland, especially in the cities of Guangzhou and Foshan. Local governments paid great attention to the development of Cantonese opera, and a number of new plays were created based on historical stories popular among local people. An excellent example of this is a series of Cantonese opera plays based on the historical figure Huang Feihong, created and performed by the Foshan Youth Cantonese Opera Troupe, including *The Tale of the Ban on Opium-Smoking* (*jin yan ji*, 《禁烟记》) and *A Tale of Fantasy* (*qi qing ji*, 《奇情记》), with the latter gaining eight awards in the Guangdong Provincial Art Festival. The Foshan Youth Cantonese Opera Troupe often gives over 100 performances in the mainland each year, and

it also gives performances in other regions
and countries including Hong Kong,
Macao, Singapore, the United States and
Canada.

Performance of *A Tale* of *Fantasy (qi qing ji)*

However, in other Chinese societies,
like Hong Kong, economic development
has brought many new forms of
entertainmens; the audience of Cantonese
opera now mostly consists of aged people,
and most young people reject it as an
outdated entertainment activity. Within
Cantonese opera circles, the training of

An English-speaking performance

young and new performers also tends to be difficult. To deal with this
challenge, Cantonese opera artists have made great efforts to reform this
ancient operatic form. The reform of language is a bold one. In 1947,
Wong Chin-wa, president of the Wah Yan Dramatic Society Limited
of Wah Yan College, Hong Kong, began to create Cantonese opera in
English, giving performances of many traditional plays of Cantonese
opera in English, including *The Perfect Match for a Military Couple*
(*jia ou bing rong*,《佳偶兵戎》), *Getting Engaged Three Times* (*yin
yuan san ding*,《姻缘叁订》), *How the Crow and Sparrow Turn
into Phoenixes* (*ya que ru he zuo feng huang*,《鸦雀如何作凤凰》)

Cantonese opera

and *Wang Zhaojun* (《王昭君》). In Singapore, Leslie Wong, president of Chinese Theatre Circle Ltd, also devoted his time and energy to the development of Cantonese opera in English; he not only performed in the play *The Eternal Regret in the Palaces of the Qing Dynasty* (*qing gong yi hen*, 《清宫遗恨》), but also created *Picking Up a Jade Bracelet* (*shi yu zhuo*, 《拾玉镯》), a Cantonese opera play in Malay, seeking to promote Chinese operatic culture all over the world. Some other artists do the same thing from the perspective of dramatic themes. In 2001, Luo Jiaying, Qin Zhongying, Wen Zhipeng and others adapted Shakespeare's *Macbeth* into a Cantonese opera play entitled *Hero of Treason* (*ying xiong pan guo*, 《英雄叛国》).

In the mainland, Cantonese opera artists have also made many efforts in various aspects, in addition to the adaption of Shakespeare's *The Merchant of Venice* into a Cantonese opera play entitled *The Daughter from a Wealthy Family* (*hao men qian jin*, 《豪门千金》). In August 2004, the first animated film in the form of Cantonese opera, *The Sassy Princess and Her Blunt Husband* (《刁蛮公主戆驸马》) was granted an Award for Outstanding Animation at the China Huabiao Film Awards. In 2008, the first Cantonese opera in the form of cosplay show, *The Butterfly Princess* (《蝴蝶公主》), was put on stage in college towns around the country, integrating elements of comic animation into Cantonese opera.